TRAINING GAMES FROM THE INSIDE

TRAINING GAMES FROM THE INSIDE

THE SECRET TO WHAT WORKS AND WHAT DOESN'T

JEFF STIBBARD

Business +
Publishing

Business + Publishing

Unit 7/5 Vuko Place
Warriewood NSW 2102
Australia
ACN 054 568 688

E-mail: info@bpp.com.au
Web site: www.bpp.com.au

© Jeff Stibbard 1998

First published 1998
Reprinted 2000

National Library of Australia
Cataloguing-in-Publication entry

   Jeff Stibbard
      Training Games ... from the inside : The secret to what
      works and what doesn't

      ISBN 1 875889 40 X.

      1. Management games – Study and teaching. 2. Teams in
      the workplace. 3. Group relations training. 4. Experiential
      learning. I. Title.

   658.40353

Publisher: Tim Edwards
Edited by Martin Heng
Printed in Australia by The Australian Print Group

Distributed in Australia and New Zealand by Woodslane Pty Limited. Business + Publishing titles are available through booksellers and other resellers. For further information contact Woodslane Australia on +61 2 9970 5111 or Woodslane Ltd, New Zealand on +64 6 347 6543, or e-mail info@bpp.com.au.

Contents

Foreword

This book is a long overdue and honest look at training games. I've spent years reading games books that focus on the gimmicky solution, or that are written by Americans, for American participants. Thankfully, this book cuts through the Americana to give you the real basis for training games, and how you can use them in your own sessions. It's a real pleasure to see such a book written by an Australian, for Australian audiences.

That Jeff Stibbard is behind this book is no surprise. Some of you reading this book may not have had the opportunity to attend one of his training workshops. Those who have, will attest to his ability not only in running games, but in making training participant-centred. In my role, I have had extensive exposure to the best trainers in Australia, and Jeff is clearly one of them, with excellent design, presentation and debriefing skills. That he is constantly booked-out speaks for itself. I am very glad that he has finally put his experience and insights on paper.

Both the quality of the games, and the insights Jeff brings to games in general, make this book a worthwhile investment. The book's approach could affect how training is presented across Australia, because it shows how to add life, add interest and avoid the dreaded 'death by overhead'. And it does so in a way that is straightforward and easy to implement. If your experience is anything like mine, I am sure you will put into practice many of the games and ideas that you pick up while reading this book.

REG POLSON
Managing Director
Polson Training Brokers

Acknowledgments

This book is based on the contributions of a vast number of people. I am grateful to all those trainers who have inspired, directly or indirectly, each of the games in this book. I cannot claim that all the games in this book are mine—but they are ones that I have seen, collected, played with and recreated over the years.

I have sought to find any original creators of games that have been passed around the Australian training community, but, as with any oral tradition, the originators can almost never be found. Consequently, I thank all those people who have unknowingly contributed to the games and variations in this book.

In particular, I'd like to thank James Falk and his writing team at Aragon Gray, and Louise Humphries. Without their support I couldn't have written this book. Finally, I would like to thank the thousands of course participants who have allowed me to put all these games into practice, and to find out what works and what doesn't.

Part I

Introduction to training games

Electrify your presentations

Thousands of people start work as trainers or presenters each year, often with little experience. They soon discover that training and presenting well is difficult to achieve. There is much to learn—presentation skills, learning theory, training design and training elements such as games. These are only a few of the areas a training wizard has to master.

Games are only a part of this training picture. But what a part they can play! Through these pages you'll see how games can lift an ordinary presentation or training session into a memorable learning experience. You'll understand why games can involve participants in a way that a talking head or high-tech presentation can't. And you'll see how to do it even if you're not a training wizard already.

Even if you're already an experienced trainer, you'll be able to use more than 50 of the best tried-and-tested games for specific training situations. You'll also be able to draw on my notes from running the actual games in the training room.

This book is more than a menu of games. The section of games is supported by an explanation of how and why games work, and what you have to do to make sure they keep working. There is some theory, but only enough to allow you to know what you're doing when you use games. This book is designed to be used, not read. Each game has notes on where it works best, possible pitfalls and variations, and strategies for getting the most out of participants. Through these notes you get access to my 10 years' experience of running games in sessions across Australia and Asia. This short-circuits the learning that you have to do—so you can pick up a game and use it like a master from the first time.

I may have collected more than 50 great games over the years; but I also know that anyone can create a great game for a specific need. I've done it the night before a training session and even during one. To be able to create a game that meets a particular learning outcome, all you need is knowledge of the basic principles of game design and a good imagination. After flicking through this book, using some of the games and reading the section on designing games, you should be in a position to create your own. I'll know I've succeeded with this book if you eventually throw it away and rely on your own imagination and skills to create games that electrify your presentations.

Introduction to the training process

Across Australia training rooms are filled with people daydreaming, or even going to sleep. Why? The reason is that many trainers think that training is only about information. It is about information in one very important way—the transfer of a skill, behaviour, insight or knowledge. But it's more than that. It's rare that what a trainer presents is groundbreaking knowledge in its own right—the information is usually available elsewhere. Rather, training is about making that information available to people in such a way that they can make it their own. Training fails, and sleep prevails, when trainers take responsibility only for the information that is being transferred. Successful trainers take responsibility for the process of learning, and in doing so bring their training to life.

As trainers we desperately need to do it. A recent study showed that 87% of information presented in training is not used in the real world (Broad and Newstrom, *The Transfer of Training*). That means that only 13% of the content of your sessions is being learnt. If we want different results from our training, we have to do something different, and we have to invest in other training procedures—procedures like the use of games. Games are the focus of this book, and they are only one of many tools available to you. But even though there are other tools, my experience has been that when well used games make a bigger difference than any other training element.

The four-step model

A simple model of this training process can help explain how learners only use that 13% of training information. This four-step model is my way of looking at what happens in the training room. There are a lot of other learning models, many of them with four steps.

In the training process, learners:

- are motivated to learn
- incorporate the new content
- apply that content
- extend the content to new areas.

Most trainers focus on the second step—delivering content so learners can incorporate it. What this ignores is that the later steps, application and extension, are what make the information truly usable. It's through these steps that people turn what they've heard into what they can do.

What's more, when trainers focus solely on incorporating content, they make that goal harder to reach. That's because applying and extending knowledge reinforces it and ensures learners incorporate it fully.

What trainers have to do in training

The key benefit of training is that it adds to people's options, rather than reconfirms their existing ones. This means that training must involve allowing the learners to recognise something new.

There are two ways to do this: we can present people's blind spots to them, so they realise that they may not know about something, or do it as well as they thought. Or we can do it covertly, by making them recognise or create the new information for themselves. In both these cases, it is the trainer's responsibility to ensure that the learners gain that new information.

Too often trainers see facilitation as the learners leading the session, and the trainer as someone who helps learners to find their own information. This isn't what training is about. If learners actually lead the session, they only reinforce their existing knowledge or inappropriate behaviours. This can be a mistake that allows participants to walk away without challenging their low skills, without expanding what options they have and without gaining from your expertise. The trainer must direct the session, even when seeming to facilitate. It's only by doing this that the trainer can ensure learners gain that information.

This entails an important ethical idea. If you as a trainer don't have something new to offer the people in front of you, something they currently don't have, you shouldn't be there. You have a responsibility to lead them to a higher skill level. Facilitation alone may make them feel good, but if all it does is reconfirm their existing options, it is a role that managers should undertake in their role as coach.

All this means that a trainer must take responsibility for leading the group somewhere new, and take that role through the training. But what has this to do with games?

Trainers have to:
- add to people's options
- take responsibility for leading people to a higher skill level
- be willing to confront learners about low skill levels
- only facilitate if this brings about something new.

Where games fit in the training process

You can present information that conclusively shows people something that they should believe or do—and get nowhere doing it. When a large part of people's behaviour—some say even 95%—is habitual and unconscious, people have to do more than just hear information. They have to engage with it, own it, and do something differently. By doing this people connect the training content with how they see the world and their role in the world. Only then will they break through those unconscious habits that govern them, and actually apply the new knowledge. That's the role of applying and extending training content. And that's the goal that successful trainers aim for and achieve. They can bring about that engagement with information through the skilled use of games.

Games do this by allowing a temporary reversal of the trainer-learner relationship. In games it is the participants who lead, rather than the trainer. Once a trainer introduces the games and the rules, it is the learners who play, and who control their own behaviours. They're in charge of what they are doing and what information they are gathering. Games then allow the learners to apply the content and see how it can be used elsewhere.

In this way games are an opportunity for the participants to engage with and integrate new content the trainer has given them. Integrating information involves taking something you know and then making it something you can do when you know it's the right thing to do. Because the participants are in charge of what they're doing, games allow them to make their own connections, and to deal with the material in their own way. This helps them to develop ownership of the material, and also helps integration.

It is in the debrief to the game that you as trainer regain control of the direction of the session and reconnect the game to new information you want to present. There are many ways to do this, and we'll discuss them in detail in a later section. For now, just remember that the debrief is your way of taking back the lead in the session and making the game a step on the path to where you want to go.

The focus of this book is on training games that can help make the last three steps in the training process work. And because applying and extending knowledge makes incorporating it a lot easier, games have the most effect when you use them to apply and extend the content you present.

Ways people can incorporate new information

Try to remember when you were at school, in a class or with a teacher that you didn't like much. What was your attitude to what you were being taught? If you were like me, you probably resented being there, and resented the information that was coming your way. Or couldn't see any point or value in it. That's a natural response to dealing with information that you are forced to hear even if you don't want to listen.

Training doesn't have to be like that. Sadly, our experience of school and other formal learning is that we are told what we need to learn, or forced to hear what we don't want to learn, and that there is no other way. Wrong! There are many ways people can gain information, and a successful trainer can tap into all those methods at the appropriate time.

One of the most useful ways of looking at how people incorporate information focuses on their point of view. This is useful because the learners' point of view determines how they approach the information you're giving them. If that attitude is positive and active, and involves them feeling in control, they're more likely to see the information as something they want to learn. And they're more likely to learn it. Let's go back to school again—where did you learn best: the class where you had some chance of controlling what you were doing, or where it was just shoved down your throat?

When we look at the learners' view of information, we can see they can come by information by:

• being forced to hear it
• being told it
• inventing it from their own resources
• discovering it somewhere else
• stealing it when it is not directed at them.*

Forced to hear

When learners are forced to attend a session by management they bring their bodies and leave their brains at the door. They have no motivation to be there, and may even have a motivation to oppose the information being presented. By being forced to hear what you are presenting, learners are stripped of any active control over their own learning. All this creates big barriers to successful training. The learners become resistant to learning anything at all and are unlikely to achieve competence in the desired skill area. Once I had to present customer focus sessions to a computing firm, and attendance was compulsory for all senior staff. Halfway through the session I found people opening bags of chips and eating, wandering in and out of the room, and talking to each other.

This can be the most challenging training assignment you can have. As a strategy for delivering information, it's a dud. I resolved this particular problem by talking about why they didn't want to be there, what that meant to them and how we could deal with it. It was a bit of a detour, but it changed the session from one in which they

---

* Adapted from Philipa Bond's Neuro-Educative Feedback Model (unpublished).

were forced to hear to one where they were able to participate. Once they were participating it was easier to guide them back to the topic of customer service.

Told

Most sessions are driven by telling. A standard lecture is a prime example. This can communicate information well, especially when it is novel information that is interesting in itself. But from the learners' point of view it is very passive. The learners may want to be there and learn the information, but they still don't have any input into what they're learning. Because the information source is completely outside them, it means they have to make more connections and do much more work to incorporate it successfully. What's more, telling sessions can easily degenerate into boring, forced-to-hear sessions when trainers deliver common sense dressed up as new information, information that is too general, or impractical advice people immediately discount.

There's no avoiding telling in training. It's a useful and successful method, but it is passive and therefore not as powerful as other ways of imparting information.

Invented

Learning that is based on invention involves the learners' creativity. When doing many things—from minor task to major project—people have to use their creativity to overcome problems. The solutions they generate are actually new information they have gained for themselves. In this way gaining information becomes something active and partially in the control of the learner. Connections are easier to make and the learner can integrate the information more easily.

When someone creates something they remember the creation as a powerful thing in their lives. They feel proud at having produced something unique. As an example, I get the same sort of feeling in doing puzzles and watching game shows—it's the pride and the thrill of making something or getting something right. It is this sense of achievement that allows people to remember more easily.

With information gained through invention, we enter higher-level learning—where gaining and retaining information is faster and longer lasting. As a trainer you can access this through setting problems that demand creative solutions.

Discovered

Learners discover information when they have to choose it from alternatives. This allows them to take a grounded, concrete approach to the subject. They may not know which option to choose straightaway, but go through a process of comparison and analysis. They test and consider and look to the future to see which option will work. As they do this they step through the process, look at it, understand it and apply it.

This way of gaining information engages the rational side of the learner. Because the source of the information they have gained is their own analysis, they incorporate and remember it much more easily.

This discovery applies to more personal learning as well. In a recent team game one group decided not to make a team presentation. What they discovered in deciding this was that a loss of face in front of the other groups was more important than participating. This choice brought up other issues each time they chose not to present something and thus allowed them a way to understand their personal process.

Stolen

Do you remember overhearing your parents speaking when you were a child? I can still remember overhearing my father telling my brother how to use a chisel. He spoke about angles and wood grain and other things I didn't really understand at the time. But I've never forgotten it, and I still hear his advice when I'm chiselling out wood. It wasn't directed at me but I listened and learnt it anyway. That's the power of stolen information.

The first way we learn is through stolen information—we all learned language by overhearing our parents. And once we have our language we take whatever information comes our way, even if it isn't directed at us. When information is directed at someone else, it is natural to think that it is important and worth something. This can be very powerful—we have a very strong urge to know what other people think is important. And because stealing the information is something we do, it is an active and self-directed way of learning. All this combines to make stealing information part of higher-level learning, and a means to remember and use information more easily.

Higher-level learning and games

Inventing, discovering or stealing information creates a higher-level learning. How does this relate to games?

Games in the training room provide a perfect means of introducing higher-level learning. Good game design can set up problems that produce invented knowledge that matches your training outcome. The same design can allow for discovered information. Stealing information is a natural part of any group activity—we can overhear or observe others and learn from what they say and do. Games provide a gateway to better incorporation and retention of information because they allow for higher-level learning. It's through games that you can overcome the limitations of simply telling people things, and boring them stiff in the process.

> **People learn at a higher level through games when they:**
> * invent information from their own resources
> * discover information from somewhere else
> * steal information when it isn't directed at them.

Fun and learning

The training process relies heavily on the relationship the trainer develops with the audience. The trust in this relationship allows the trainer to lead people where they wouldn't usually go, and to develop new beliefs and new habits.

Now, while all learning isn't fun, there is a connection between enjoyment and learning. When an audience is laughing, they tend to trust and identify more with the presenter and with the other participants. Learners share the common experience of laughter, and this common experience helps build a relationship with other learners. Equally, people respond positively to trainers who make them laugh, and are more willing to make allowances for the unavoidable errors and generalisations of training.

You can build this sort of strong relationship with your audience in many ways. You may have already met ideas of building rapport or getting to know your audience. This involves establishing a kind of contact and trust between the trainer and learners. The reason I have focused on fun is that I believe it is the most effective way of building this relationship, and I know that it offers additional benefits.

You can tell immediately if you have successfully introduced fun into your sessions. How? By the obvious evidence of laughter. When there is laughter in the room you know you have established a good training relationship, you know you are on the way to good relationships among learners, and you know that you will be able to lead the learners to a new place.

Fun, in all its forms, increases the energy level in the training. This means people are more positive, more responsive and more alert. It also changes the state of the learner, and helps ensure they associate that change with some new information.

And fun can allow you to introduce games in a way that is less scary for those learners who look on games with fear. When people are laughing in their seats, they have a relationship with the trainer and other learners, and they are likely to feel more comfortable getting out of their seats with a smile on their face. There is no need for games to scare any participant. It simply requires that you establish not only a relationship with learners, but a relationship based in fun.

What this means is that team building is a built-in part of every program you run— by using fun, groups, games and activities you allow learners to work together five or six times a day. Team building follows automatically, no matter what the training subject, because there is a relationship already established and no hierarchy in the training room. People share experiences in a trusting environment. What better team building could there be?

Key ideas in the training process:
- Training involves motivation, incorporation, application and extension.
- Trainers have a responsibility to lead.
- Games improve incorporation, application and extension.
- Games lead to higher-level learning.
- Games help learning by introducing fun.

What are training games?

Games are notoriously difficult to define in general. But for us, it's only games in the training room that are really important. In the training room, games are a discovery exercise where people learn by participative experience. This means that in the process of the game, learners find out something that they didn't know previously. The way they find this out is by:

- doing an activity
- reflecting on what they did
- making connections between what they know, what they've done, and the real world.

This takes learners further along the training process toward applying and extending what they've learnt.

For this to work, the game has to be structured in a way that ensures learners discover what you want them to discover. And most importantly, you have to guide the process of reflection so that they identify the connections that you want them to. I look at this guidance in more detail when I discuss debriefing.

What training games have in common with other games

There must be a goal set for the game. This is what the participants aim towards in playing the game. It may be solving a puzzle, or finding a partner, or whatever. If there is no goal, the game becomes an experiential exercise that can go in any direction. The participants can make of it what they will. This can be of benefit in some circumstances, but not in the games situation in the training room. In any game, if there is no goal, participants have no guidance on how to act. Imagine playing football when there was no way either team could score tries or goals. What would be the point?

This goal is different from the training outcome you have for the game. The training outcome is your idea of what you want people to get out of the game. You don't have to tell the learners the training outcome—and in most cases you shouldn't. But you must tell the learners the goal of the game itself.

Games are timebound. This means they have a clear start and finish time. Not only is this important for the scheduling of your sessions, but it also increases participants' focus on the game. It can also motivate activity if there is some sort of race against the clock.

Games may have challenges or obstacles that match or relate to real challenges in the world of work. The game challenges are a metaphor for what the participants encounter in the real world, and allow them to apply the content of the session in a way that shows how it works.

Rules are essential to games. When you are managing a group of people there has to be a realistic set of guidelines for their activity. This ties in with the goal for the game. These guidelines can be minimal, but they must allow for the process to work effectively. Rules at least have to:

- set the outcome, time and challenges of the game
- specify what conduct is not allowed
- establish the nature of the relationships among the players.

Within the rules you also have to include a clear way of finishing the game. It is essential to have a clear finish to allow you to manage your session, and to debrief in a way that allows learners to gain meaning from the game. If there is no clear termination to the game, you can lose control and it can become an experiential exercise that can wander.

Lastly, a key element is that games are fun. If we forgot this we'd leave out the most important part of the idea. Fun is what makes games different from a work project you've got to finish by five o'clock or from a procedure in an industrial plant. Fun is the defining element of games.

All games have:
- a goal
- time limits
- challenges or obstacles
- rules
- a clear finish point
- fun as an essential element.

What's special about training games

Training games have to be aligned to the content of the training. There has to be a point to the game, and a point that is relevant to the topic. That point can be simply to have fun. But a point there has to be and people have to realise it. People don't like wasting their time, and a game for its own sake does just that. Both their and your time is too important to waste, so don't treat that time disrespectfully by playing games that don't have a clear purpose. Learners are pretty insightful and they'll know if what you're doing is a piece of fluff, or if it is relevant. You also have to make sure that you say how it is relevant, or that you will explain how it is relevant later. I cover this aspect of the introduction further when I discuss running games.

In games the role of the trainer and learner are reversed. The participant takes control of what's happening within the game's rules, and how they play. This more dominant role allows learners to take more ownership of what's happening. If there isn't a change of lead in the session, participants will only be going through the motions in the game. This stops them from taking any responsibility for where they are going and undermines the value of the activity. When this happens you tend to get a lot of pointless or childish questions about rules or behaviours. These appear when people are struggling against taking responsibility for the game or for their own learning. Recognising and dealing with this is important, and again we'll meet this issue when we look at running games.

But remember: training games are fun, and are also more than just fun. They provide information, illustrate ideas and show applications. But they do all that while being fun at the same time.

Training games:
- are aligned to training content
- provide an illustration or application of that content
- give the lead back to the learners
- introduce fun to the training session.

Games compared with other exercises

Games used in training differ from other activities, such as simulations, role plays, and experiential and computer exercises.

Simulations and role plays usually try to create some significant aspect of a real situation, or set up a chance to implement a realistic solution. This involvement with simulated reality makes them different from training games focused on learning. For example, you could simulate dealing with a difficult customer in a service training session. This simulation allows people to apply their new-found knowledge, but it isn't a game. There's no fun. There's little in the way of rules or outcomes—it's just practice and pretend reality.

Experiential exercises are activities where people can draw their own conclusions from the sort of experience they go through. Often the activity may not be clearly aligned to any training outcome. It may run for a very long time and involve challenges that are present merely because they are challenges. Abseiling is a classic example of an outdoor experiential exercise.

Experiential exercises and simulations usually require a greater time commitment, and are more complex to set up, run and interpret. Often, they also involve more dangerous situations and need much more equipment.

Games differ in that they provide an element of fun, surprise or excitement often lacking in the other types of exercises. This is because they provide a change in state or tempo from one section to the next in the training process. While role plays and simulations allow learners to apply knowledge, it is in the same emotional and mental state as the learning. The benefit of moving from incorporation to exploration to application is maximised when there is a change in state for each step. Games provide that change.

Characteristics of a good game

Good training games are:

- brief
- inexpensive
- involving for the participants
- low risk, with proven success
- adaptable to different situations
- simple to play and supervise
- non-threatening
- focused on a single outcome.

What games can do

We've looked at what training is, how people learn best and where games fit in the training process. What you now need to know is what exactly games do in helping people to incorporate, apply and extend their knowledge or skills. Armed with this you'll be able to work out when and how a game can be a solution to a training problem.

> **The Magnificent Seven**
> There are seven powerful ways you can use training games:
> - Put learners in the right place to learn.
> - Make the learning concrete.
> - Make a bridge between knowledge and action.
> - Help learners reach higher-level learning.
> - Produce creative solutions.
> - Allow monitoring of learning.
> - Change pace and energy.

Put learners in the right place to learn

Presenting people content gives them a capability to do something. It does not necessarily mean that they *want* to do it. As a trainer you have to address their beliefs and values in such a way that they want to put that capability into action. You can do this through a well-designed game and a structured debrief after the game. Not only do games allow for new angles on particular information, they also allow you to draw people to view the world in general from new angles.

Learner suspicion and lack of interest can undermine any training session. Games are one means of overcoming these problems.

If the content really challenges the learner's beliefs and represents quite a big step for them, a game can be a safe way of easing into it. What may seem weird to a participant in the real world is more acceptable when experienced through a game. In this way participants can experience the solution without the emotional danger—and actually see that it works.

Make the learning concrete

Games are a way of taking what you *know*, and making it something you can *do*. In games the participants can make their own connections and deal with the material in their own way, which makes it real for them.

Participants integrate material better through games because they involve more of our senses. When we sit and listen to a lecture, generally we are using our hearing and, if we're lucky, our sight. But these are only two of the ways we relate to the world. In games, we involve ourselves through other ways as well. Games may involve physical movement, touch, speech, visualisations and memory. These allow the learner to make different and broader associations with the material. As a trainer you may be hard pressed to create a game using taste and smell, but even with this limitation you are way ahead of the boring lecture. Remember: more senses, more learning.

In the same way games relate the training to the world outside the training room. A game can be a metaphor for the real world—as people see the application of the training content in the game, it can help them to see the application in their own work. And if that game takes the participants out of their comfort zone and challenges their beliefs, it's a lot easier for them to transfer new beliefs to the real world.

Real life often differs from training in that everything happens at the same time. In order for people to learn, training information is often simplified into a separated linear sequence. Because the real world doesn't always follow things step-by-step, it's important learners can deal with the information in a dynamic way. Games are dynamic—they can relate to many things in time at the same time, and they move and change.

Games also address *how* the content works. Most trainers spend a lot of time on the content, on what you're supposed to do. But how you do it is just as important. Games can demonstrate how things work in a concrete way, and this in its turn affects the content itself—by seeing how it works, the content also becomes clearer.

Make a bridge between knowledge and action

A key problem in training is that people often lack options about *how* to do what they want to do. They know what they should do in principle—but what they lack is the capacity to break their established habit. They have the knowledge but find it difficult to act on that knowledge. It's a common problem with many names. In our personal world we might call it laziness or procrastination. In the corporate world we might call it resistance to change. But in the training room it's a barrier to learning. It's here that games can act as a bridge between knowledge and action. Because games involve activity, you can use them to link action to the information in the training session. Through this link, through using games as a bridge, you can help people to break habitual barriers to using their knowledge.

Help learners reach higher-level learning

When I talked about higher-level learning, I explained how inventing, discovering and stealing information helped people incorporate and retain information better. Games provide the best means to allow your learners to do this. Through games learners can create solutions to problems, compare and analyse options and encounter information not directed to them. Provided the games are designed with the session outcomes in mind, they can ensure that learners deal with the training content in an engaged and interested way.

Produce creative solutions

When you have prepared the participants to take the lead in the session, they may then produce options and answers you may not have anticipated. Although it's your responsibility to bring something new to the training room, the process of training can spark remarkable insights in your participants. It's a fact of life as a trainer that you deal with people who know an enormous amount, much more than you could ever know. If the content has been well explained, when participants get the opportunity to lead their own learning they can produce highly creative solutions.

Creative answers also appear during games as relationships strengthen among participants. These stronger relationships develop because games create a common experience for the group, and common experience is the basis for many relationships. As the relationships develop, many powerful new ideas can come from peers, and from the way participants can 'spark' off one another.

Allow monitoring of learning

Games also provide an opportunity for the trainer to see how well learners have integrated the information presented. If, in the process of a game, the participants demonstrate the behaviours or content you've presented, you know that they have learnt it and integrated it. If not, you know you will have to take back the leading role in the debrief and redirect them until they do. Most games are like this. Very few learners can integrate content and demonstrate it in a single game, especially when the training group and the trainer may be relative strangers. Because of this, taking back the lead and taking the learners further along the path to new information is vitally important to games. We look at this in detail in the section on debriefing games.

Change pace and energy

Attention is important to learning. Learners are limited as to how much attention they can give to the same topic presented in the same way. Some studies suggest attention starts to wander after 17–20 minutes of the same form of presentation. Games can provide identifiable breaks in routine and tempo for learners. This helps maintain an atmosphere of freshness, enthusiasm and engagement. All this ensures higher levels of attention and better learning.

Games help overcome one of the greatest and most common learning disorders—boredom. We've already seen how little information people use from their training, and how quickly they can lose interest, so it's very important that you address boredom in your training design. Because games involve a change in what learners are doing, they can help to short-circuit boredom.

Because games change how people feel and what they do (their *state*), they are a good marker for the stages in the training process. People remember better when they can associate information with changes in pace, energy and state. For this reason, when moving from incorporation of information to application or extension, a game can help learning by changing the learners' state.

Pitfalls in using games

Games are both emotionally and educationally powerful. This is their strength and their weakness. When you are using games you have to be sure that participants are in the right place to respond to them in the right way, and that you present and run them in the right way. If you don't, you can easily generate the wrong learning outcome or end up annoying your learners. With this in mind, there are several pitfalls to look out for.

Giving too much information about the game

You can spend too much time going over the game in detail, or explaining its principles, or telling people what they will get out of it. If you do this, you can spoil the process of the game and make it impossible to tell if learners have really got anything out of it.

We talked about the power of discovered, stolen and invented information earlier. If you talk too much about the game or its outcome, you end up telling people what they may have invented, discovered or stolen for themselves. This can undermine the benefits that made you choose the game in the first place. Of course you should guide the attention of the learners by suggesting the types of outcomes they may meet—this helps to create a high-level debrief and higher-level learning. But if you baldly state the outcome, it can be counterproductive.

We also said that games are a way of checking that learners have grasped the content. If you tell them too much, or talk about the outcome, they can just produce the result without engaging in the process, or even understanding it.

The answer here is the same as for the previous two problems—give learners as much information as they need to see that the game is relevant and to enable them to play the game well. This amount can change from group to group and game to game. It's up to you as a trainer to monitor how the learners respond and give more or less information accordingly.

Unrealistic expectations of the game

I'm sure your parents used to do what mine did—whenever there was anything I didn't want to do, they'd tell me that I'd love it, it'd be great, it was the best. Of course it wasn't. And that just made it worse.

Being realistic and truthful is just as important when you are introducing a game and trying to reassure people. If you introduce a game as being easy and fun, and it later proves difficult, you lose the trust you have established. Learners can think that they're dumb, and they won't want to engage in any other games you suggest.

You're better off being honest about the game. If it's difficult, don't build it up as impossible, but let them know a little of what to expect. It's fair on the learners and it ensures their trust for future games.

Group not ready for the game or can't see the point

One of the biggest problems with games is when they are sprung on learners who haven't been made ready for them. One of the responsibilities of the trainer is to build the trust and generate the energy that will allow learners to accept games. We've already touched on this in what trainers have to do and how to use fun and learning. If you just dump a game on your learners without leading them to the right place, they will reject the game.

We look at how to lead learners to the right place in the section on introducing games.

Learners already played the game

Some of the best training games are known by most trainers. It's likely that sometimes you will start a game and someone will pipe up and say that they played it last week with another trainer.

If it is only one person, for some games you could continue anyway. But if you have a fair number who have already played the game, run another one. If you play the same game it will only key into what happened in the other session and obscure your objective. And those that haven't played the game won't get much out of it because they will watch those that have. It pays to prepare a back-up game just in case.

Recently I set up to play a game that relies on people making one of five animal sounds. Just as I'd started, I realised that a person in the room was mute, and couldn't play. I had two options: to go ahead, and make him an observer, or stop and set up an alternative game. I set up an alternative, because he had already been an observer in a previous game.

It's important to remember that bad games can also carry memories of bad training. This is especially true of mediocre openers—the 'I'm John and I want to learn communication skills' snore-fests. If possible find out if anyone has had bad game experiences before you start the session.

Implying games are a waste of time

The last thing you should do is play a game as a filler. Introducing a game with 'Let's play a game to take us to lunch' is a certain way of telling your audience that what you're doing is irrelevant and unimportant. It's hard enough convincing people that games are a useful tool without cutting your own throat by doing something like this.

If you treat games with disrespect and pop them into gaps in a session without making them relevant, your learners will be disrespectful too. But they will treat all your games that way, even ones that are central to your sessions. Doing anything in the training room without respect for your learners or your credibility will come back and bite you.

To ensure learners approach games knowing that they are important:

- at the start of the day, explain how games in general will relate to the content presented
- refer back to this set-up during the day before any games
- explain how any individual game is relevant.

Groups finish the tasks at different speeds

When you have several groups playing a game, some groups can be quicker than others. If you ignore this, the groups that finish faster or understand better will quickly disrupt the other learners. This is also a problem when one group is simply uninterested in any applications of training content, and wants to move on to the next part of the game.

You have to address this. You can manage the early finishers by asking them to:

- run a small debrief for their group only
- split up and join other groups
- do an advanced or another task
- give you general feedback on the session or the day.

You have to recognise their achievement of finishing early. Make them feel they have done something extraordinary. By asking their opinion or asking them to help other groups, you validate that achievement. Not only does this make them feel good about the game, it builds rapport and makes them more likely to support you and respond to the remainder of the session.

What you must *not* do is tell them to go and get another cup of coffee, or to go for a walk. Although this is easy for you, it doesn't recognise their success, it allows them to lose focus and distracts the other learners. In fact, you are punishing the early finishers by sending them away.

Giving the impression you are doing something unplanned

I have presented in a very flexible and responsive way, only to have learners suggest that I should present a more structured program. Even though the program was highly structured, because I was flexible and relaxed about what I was doing, the learners had the impression that I was making it up as I went along. Because of this they thought the games I presented were a waste of time.

The important thing here is to ensure that your learners know that games are part of a structured approach to training, not something to fill in time. It is also important to be *seen* to present in a structured way simply to maintain your professional reputation. Sometimes I even refer to training notes when I don't need to—simply so people know I am on a path that is designed to go somewhere.

Group too rowdy or enthusiastic

Sometimes a group can become too enthusiastic about a game. This is a particular problem at late-night conferences and when alcohol may be involved. Single-gender groups also tend to get more out of control than mixed groups.

The group can over-respond to the music and humour that you use, or may just want to fool around. They can become over-enthusiastic and over-energised. Learners may be looking forward to finishing, or you may have a bad training environment with a lot of distractions. If this is the case, they won't listen to instructions and they won't put a value on the game or draw any lessons from it. You will lose the connection to the real world. The motto is—always monitor your group and the direction they are taking. If they are already rowdy a game may not be the tool to use. If they are becoming rowdy during a game, you have to change their state and take back control.

You can wind back this over-response by:

- using slower and quieter music
- lowering and slowing down your voice
- being very directive and controlling all aspects of the game
- getting people to report to the entire group so everyone has to stop and listen
- not using partners or small groups where you can't supervise everyone at once.

Associations with a previous session

There are many things about games and about training that can carry over from other sessions. Often the things people remember from boring training sessions are the type of mints, the coffee cups, the pens and stationery. Be aware that doing something different for these things allows you to separate your training from those bad memories. The same applies to games. Playing a game can drag up memories of other bad sessions. What you have to do is remind people that this is a different game, run by a different trainer.

When to use games

As part of any session plan

Because games are a powerful tool to help learners incorporate, explore and apply content, they can be an essential part of any session. Session planning is a particular skill and there are a lot of books and courses devoted to it. The important thing to remember is that games are useful in most stages of the learning process, and are always useful in changing the state of learners who may lose interest every 20 minutes or so.

Games are another training tool you can plan to use, just like the lecture, chalk-and-talk, simulations, case studies and so on.

Lack of interest and energy

You can use games to counter a gradual decline in interest or to help struggling learners grasp the content you're presenting. This is a key issue. When you see that learners are drifting into a 'comatose' state you have to intervene, otherwise you'll lose them.

This is where an ad hoc game that may not be in your session plan can help. Such a game is a way of controlling the state the learners are in, and keeping them in a good place to learn.

This makes it your responsibility as a trainer to monitor your audience, and to be flexible and prepared to incorporate a game in different places. And you can only do that if you're looking for the signs that your learners are lagging.

How you can tell when learners are lagging

There are several key indicators that your learners are slipping into a state that makes learning difficult:

- you can see a dull look
- learners lose eye contact with you while you are presenting
- learners make a micro-movement of pushing their chairs away from the front of the room
- learners talk among themselves, or focus on eating or doodling
- learners avoid answering, or when they do answer they run on for a very long time (because they are bored)
- learners tidy their desks or put things in colour order—because it is one of the few things they can do while you are presenting.

In extreme cases you can have people standing up and walking out of the room, making mobile phone calls, getting coffee and so on. This is particularly true when you are presenting to high-level staff who are used to running sessions, not being part of them.

Have games up your sleeve

All this requires you to have some games available so you can slip them in unexpectedly. These can be games that need no preparation, or you could have the preparation on hand just in case. Either way, you've got to have a few things in your arsenal to call on when you need them. If you don't, you won't be able to control the learning state of the people you are training.

Likely times to use games

The first priority for placing games in your sessions is that they fit with your overall session plan and learning outcomes. Provided that you keep this in mind, there are some other clear times when games are useful.

In the first 10 minutes

At the beginning of a training program, a day, or a session, you can use a game to establish the tone, energy and relationship you want with the group. This time is very important for all training, whether or not you use games.

This is especially true if you are following another trainer—you pay the price for any bad trainer that goes before you. You can follow another session and find all the learners bored and thinking about being anywhere but in the training room. A game is a good way of breaking the established pattern.

Recently I followed a technical trainer who had bored the audience with two hours of overheads on a credit management system. I recognised straightaway that they had to change state if they were going to get anything out of my material. As an opener I played the Apple and Straw Game (see page 90), which generated a lot of energy and enthusiasm, and meant that my time and preparation weren't wasted.

The danger of launching into a game like the Apple and Straw straightaway is that you haven't had a chance to establish a trusting relationship. That means any game you choose has to keep the learners comfortable and contribute to trust rather than rely on it.

20 minutes before morning tea

The period leading up to morning tea can often be very flat. People are over their initial curiosity, and you've probably started content. By playing a game before morning tea, you lift the energy level for the break, create relationships that get strengthened over the break and help learners give each other feedback about the session. These factors result in learners returning to the training room on a slight high. Coffee and sugar can only add to this effect.

Split over lunch

You can split a game over the lunch break as a variation. Introduce it before lunch, then re-introduce it and play after lunch. This gives you some strong benefits:

- you go over the instructions twice
- learners have a game to look forward to after lunch, rather than dry content
- learners are more likely to return on time, and to be focused on the training
- learners look forward to the game, which increases their potential response to it.

Although this is useful, there are some catches. Because you give learners extra time to think about the game, there's more chance they will reject it and come back with prepared resistance.

The reverse can also be a problem. An enthusiastic group can want to play the game immediately, not after lunch. This forces you to play a 'tough teacher' and refuse them, which can undermine your relationship. Here, as elsewhere, the key to success is monitoring your audience *before* you start the game.

At the end of the day

A game at the end of the day is particularly powerful because it is the last thing the learners do, and the most likely thing they will remember from the session. Games last thing allow you to:

• close any open questions or make any links that may be missing
• see if the group has actually changed their behaviours following the training
• make a contrast between the start and the end of the day
• set up positive energy for the first session of any following day
• create a lasting positive impression of you as a trainer, that learners take away or record on evaluation sheets.

The last item might seem a little self-serving. It certainly shouldn't be the only reason you run a game. But we have to accept that as trainers often our continuing success depends on the evaluations we receive. The easiest way to receive a good evaluation is to be a good trainer: to prepare and structure the sessions well, to build and monitor relationships, to be a good performer. But even if you do all this, at the end of a long day people may feel a little negative. A game to finish is a way of protecting your reputation from an evaluation by tired learners.

Likely topics for games

If you become familiar with how games work you should be able to create relevant games for almost any topic. However, it may not be appropriate to use a game for some topics. Where the content of your training is of a grave nature, or where you don't want a sense of fun, a game would not be a good training tool. For example, in training on grief counselling or safety it is not the time to introduce a high-energy, high-laughter game. Games, and the tone of the training, must always be appropriate to audience and situation.

But these cases are rare. Simply because a topic is dull doesn't mean you can't use a game. With boring topics it is a challenge to you as a presenter to use games meaningfully. It's easy to run a fun communications skills game—it's a lot harder to make a game relevant to something like strategic planning. I had to do that for a conservative insurance company, and created a game to show the benefits of having strategy rather than none. It's described later in the book as the Noughts and Crosses game (see page 92).

How to run games

All training has to begin with a session plan that addresses the outcomes you want from the training. There are many ways of structuring training and many theories about how you should do it. All these theories stress that the training design be focused on a clear outcome. In this, as in every field, outcome and goal setting are central. Clear outcomes ensure you have both a design target and a standard for training performance.

We are interested in running games within the framework of one of these structured session plans. What you have to do to run a game is much the same as for any face-to-face learning activity. When you deal with people you have to be ready to let them know where they're going, how to do what they're doing and what it means. It's exactly the same for games, where you have to:

- prepare for playing the game
- introduce the game to the participants
- play the game
- debrief the game.

What makes a good game great

There are straightforward guidelines for each of the above steps. But to run a game as well as the best professional trainers, you also have to develop observation skills and flexibility. These skills help ensure your games meet participant needs, from preparation to debrief. As a successful trainer you have to be able to:

- shift into the participants' perspective and understand their experience
- notice everything participants do and say
- be able to change your training direction to match what you notice.

This gives you the capacity to know and understand your audience, and to adjust your games to get the maximum benefit. It may take time to learn how to monitor everything that is happening in the training room, but you can learn it. It requires concentration, awareness and a genuine interest in what is happening. It helps to trust your peripheral vision and whatever snippets you overhear.

Taking those observations and immediately doing something different requires confidence and preparation. Responding in the moment to different feedback from learners is much easier when you have thought out the possibilities and responses in advance. This sort of preparation builds your confidence and allows you to be the sort of trainer who can take control of a moment and make it memorable.

Preparing for the game

Preparation involves anything you have to do before you start telling people about the game.

Seven Steps in Preparation
1 Review your session plan
2 Identify where and why you want games in the session.
3 Choose a game that best suits the outcome you want.
4 Practice and review the game until you are thoroughly familiar with it.

5 Investigate and review:
  • the audience
  • the training, playing and debriefing environments
  • any pitfalls or problems that may arise
  • any handouts, flip charts or other materials needed.
6 Create relevant debrief questions related to the training content.
7 Ensure you have an alternative game in case of problems.

Insert a game to suit your session plan and training outcome

Preparation begins with identifying where in the session plan a game would be appropriate. You have to look to see if a game can make a contribution to your training outcome, if it can help the pacing of the session, if it can help learners stay fresh—whether any of the benefits of games can help you achieve what you want to achieve with the training. The key is to identify exactly what you want to achieve in the session and exactly how the game can help.

Choose your game

Once you've worked out where in the session you want your games, you have to find games that are appropriate for those spots. By knowing exactly what you want to achieve, you can find the game to do it. Choose one on the basis of the learning outcome you desire and the type of interaction you want to generate. Now, there are many games that can serve the same function—there are hundreds of icebreakers or communication games or observation games, for example. This book can point you in the right direction for such games, but you shouldn't confine yourself to it—there is always extra useful information out there. The important thing is to choose the game that fits your session best. It may suit the subject matter, the audience, the time available or your presentation style.

Whatever the reason, ensure you choose the one that will work best, rather than the one that is most familiar. For example, in this book there are two paper plane games with very different outcomes—one is a listening exercise, the other reveals creative thinking. Don't just throw in a game because you've always used it. If you do that you run the risk of making learners feel like you're wasting time, because they'll know you've just thrown it in and that it isn't the best way to deal with the material.

Get familiar with the game

After you've chosen your game the hard work begins. You have to be familiar with the game. Do a dummy run. Sit down and work out where things might go wrong. Make a list of materials and the sort of training environment necessary. Call up your peers who may have run the game and ask advice. And there's always the presenter's standby—present it to your partner, flatmate or parent, who can be a very tough audience and often highlight things you miss.

If you aren't familiar with the game the session will be a difficult one. Umming and erring and not knowing what you are doing in front of a group is embarrassing—and for a trainer it is both unprofessional and unfair to your learners. If you can't manage the game effectively then they have little chance of understanding the instructions, let alone making useful connections to the real world. Becoming familiar with the game is an absolutely essential step.

Get to know the audience and environment

If possible have a look at the training space a few days before the session. Work out where in the room people can play the game, where they can debrief, what games you can't play because the space isn't right. Having the right space is important for both playing and debriefing games. The play space has to allow learners to feel comfortable when playing. A different space for playing and debriefing also helps establish a different state for learners. With this in mind, work out if you need to change the layout of the room for the game, and allow time for it in your session. Consider storage for any game props, and whether the desks are the right size for what you are trying to do.

Find out how many learners there will be and make sure you have enough room, props and debrief space for them.

At the same time you can check up on your audience. Talk to your contact arranging the training, or the training manager. Find out what sort of training experience your audience has had. Any horror stories? Any feedback on games being fun, inappropriate, irrelevant or the best part of the day? Be polite, but be nosy. This is especially important if someone has been embarrassed previously when playing games—if you find this, take extra care to set up the game so that you show there is no chance of people being hurt.

Thinking about your audience allows you to foresee many of the issues that might come up unexpectedly in the game. The sort of things you need to consider include:

- bad relations between participants
- management problems leading to mistrust and worker suspicion
- learner fears of public speaking or physical activity
- learners being dressed inappropriately for the game
- illiterate or innumerate learners, or learners whose English is poor.

This list could go on forever. When you have identified your audience, you'll be able to recognise the sort of issues that might apply. Once you have an idea of any of these problems, you can alter the game to take them into account. For example, one leadership game I played involved learners standing on desks giving orders. It worked well in an industrial environment where everyone wore overalls—but in an office where people dress differently it was totally inappropriate. I changed it so that the role of the absolute ruler was indicated by a crown. It was a better version of the game for any environment.

You can keep learning more about your audience till the very last minute. If you are concerned about a game (or any part of the session) you can always speak casually to participants the day before, early on the training day, or even at morning tea and lunch. Every contact you have with the learners is an opportunity to find out how they may respond to something. You don't have to talk about any specific game, just about training issues in general. Be genuinely interested in your participants and they will volunteer a lot of what you need to know.

Prepare the concrete steps

You have to spend time creating the nuts and bolts of the game. Decide how you are going to give instructions. Prepare handouts or flip charts and group the instructions to four or five steps. This is important because most people can only remember an average of 7 +/- 2 items. Any more than this and it overflows from short-term memory. The average is seven items, and many people can only handle five. On the principle that you should pitch to the lowest number so everyone can remember the instructions, keep it to five or less.

Produce handouts, manuals, props and rewards several days before you need them. There is nothing more stressful than typing things up at the last minute and then finding in your rush you have made fewer than you need. I know that's easier said than done—I do things at the last minute too—but if you're concerned about your games it's one way to make things easier.

Plan the layout of the room or groups for the game. It ensures you won't stand in front of the room wondering about how to arrange desks and chairs, or what groups to get into. Knowing what you're doing in advance means that you both look and are professional.

Prepare your debrief structure and questions before the game. The debrief is the key learning time for participants, and here you have to connect the game to the learning outcome. Use guided questions that explore what happened, how people felt and how people can use the learning in real life.

Prepare yourself

Lastly, be prepared to react and adjust. Part of your training job is a performance, and that is especially true when you are running games. Any performance feeds off the audience and their responses. If you are ready to act on these responses to change the game plan or its presentation, you can produce a better outcome. It pays to be aware of those opportunities.

You also have to prepare your own energy and personal presentation. It's important to know what sort of energy you should have at different stages of the game, when you should melt into the background and when you should be visible to everyone. Think through what *you* have to do at every stage of the game, as well as what the participants have to see you doing.

Introducing the game

The introduction is the way you let people know where they're going and what they have to do. It's also when you have to generate enthusiasm for the game and show people that it is worthwhile that they make an effort.

> **Steps in introducing a game**
> 1 Build energy and enthusiasm.
> 2 Appeal to values.
> 3 Focus concentration on the instructions.
> 4 Give short, clear instructions.
> 5 Make learners feel safe to play the game.
> 6 Monitor audience reactions to the introduction.
> 7 Short-circuit any pitfalls and overcome any reluctance.
> 8 Offer a choice to opt out if there are insoluble problems.

With a good introduction, you set up your game for success. That's because the introduction sets the learner expectation and energy level for the game, and gives the learners what they need to play it. The learners can then play the game and get something out of it even if other elements of the game aren't as good as they could be. Learners are very resourceful—if you give them a good reason for doing something they will find connections you may not have seen. However, the real value of the game comes in the debrief, and no matter how good your introduction it can't make up for a faulty review of what people have learnt.

Build energy and enthusiasm

When you set up a game, it is important to lift your own energy and enthusiasm and work to lift those of the learners. This process is important because you have to convince them that the game is going to be fun and worth them investing time and effort. There are specific behaviours you can use to set the energy level higher. You can:

- move more rapidly around the room
- use louder and faster music
- move into the learners' space, and break down the normal spaces that trainers and learners keep to
- speak more quickly than you would normally
- clown around
- use bigger and noisier gestures, such as clapping your hands, using spread-arm and upward-moving gestures
- take a couple of steps away from the position you would normally present in, so learners can associate your new energy with a different place
- light up your face with a sincere smile.

Because all people, even learners, naturally tend to match the behaviours you present them, this will help to generate energy which will flow through to the game. In this way you can motivate your learners to involve themselves. As we discussed earlier, this process will be much easier if you have already established an atmosphere of fun and trust.

You also have to motivate them by appealing to their emotions or values. When you *explain* why you play the game, you appeal to learners' rational side. But people act on both rational and emotional grounds, so you have to plug into their values as well. This is not simple. It involves you monitoring your audience to work out the sort of values and beliefs that are predominant in the group. As with most of the theory behind training and group behaviour, there is a huge range of theories about values— the thing is to notice what your audience seems to think is important. For example, they may be motivated mainly by reward (money or material things), by power (position and decision making), by security, by community well-being and so on. There may be a great range of values in your group. But if they are a group from the same corporate culture then they are likely to have similar values. You have to develop a feel for your audience and relate the game and the learning from the game to what they see as important.

Here are some simple examples. To motivate a group of salespeople, you could describe how a game will give them insights into improving their sales or commissions. To motivate a group of older workers concerned about job security, you could explain how the game will give them skills to make them more valuable employees or more saleable in the workforce. The important thing is to get to know what is important to the audience and to use it to make the game more attractive.

When you build enthusiasm you also have to focus the learners' concentration. You need to do this before you give the instructions to ensure they listen and understand. Telling them to concentrate won't do the trick. A better way is by telling a story about a game where someone did something funny or odd because they didn't listen. If the story gets them laughing, their attention is with you.

Explain why you're playing the game

We've already looked at the importance of treating your learners with respect and of not seeming like you are wasting their time. You have to make them feel that the game is relevant to what they are doing and that they will get something out of it. This is a way of *rationally* motivating people to play. It is also a way of avoiding a common pitfall, where people can't see the point of what they are doing.

An easy way is to explain how games have made a difference in other training sessions. Success stories are hard to argue with.

I made the mistake of not explaining a game for a group that included the managing director who hired me. After about five minutes of the game, he stood up and said 'We're paying you too much money for you to be wasting time on stuff like this.' I put that in quotes because I can still remember every word, and I can still feel the heat on my face. That's a classic example of not leading your audience where you want them to go, not explaining, and paying the price.

When you explain the relevance of a game, you only have to give learners sufficient information to make the game meaningful. You should always allow some scope for them to discover the application and power of the game. This means you may have to slightly undervalue the game when you introduce it. If you explain in too much detail it can kill the outcome you are looking for.

Exactly how do you make a game relevant? What you have to give is a reason for doing it. You can state the reason in general terms, so that the learners still get to discover the specifics. For example, you could say that a game will show the basic features of teamwork, and leave it to the learners to identify those features.

Or you can give the outcome of the game if you want. Often people absorb the ideas you list in the introduction and then regurgitate them as their own ideas in the debrief. This is particularly useful with less sophisticated audiences. The problem is that it can make the game less interesting and can limit discovered knowledge.

I once introduced a game with 'You can use this approach in the workplace, at home and on the sports field.' In the debrief I asked 'What else can you get from this example?' One learner frowned, obviously thinking hard, and then discovered another application. 'Oh yeah, I was just thinking I could use this with my wife when we're at home ...'

With more sophisticated and critical audiences, you can explain games as a useful device for bringing the real world into the limited world of training room. Explain that games are specially designed to look at things in a way you can apply to the world. If you have a good relationship with the audience, they'll accept that.

If all else fails, and the audience simply cannot see why they should play the game, talk about the benefits of games we've looked at in this book. Treat them as training equals and explain the process to them. At the very least they'll learn about training games and feel flattered that you have included them in the process itself.

Give the game instructions

Learners need some basic information before they can play a game effectively. This information includes the point of the game and the instructions for the game.

The best way to communicate these instructions is to write them down, in four or five steps, and display them in places people will be able to see them. This could be on flip charts, handouts or around the wall. As you speak about the instructions people can follow and link ideas to the written steps. This is important because people tend to forget instructions, especially when groups start having fun. In any case, instructions have to be simple, clear and accessible.

The roles learners have to play are the first thing they need to know. In any game people have to act in abnormal ways, to take on a role for the game. You have to explain what that role is. It could be that they are managers who don't communicate, or game show contestants. Or they could simply be playing the role of people introducing themselves. You have to let people know who they are supposed to be, how they must act and how they are motivated in the game. Even in a fun game like The Bum Race (see page 120) people have to know how they are supposed to act.

Closely related to roles are the rules. The rules state the limits of the behaviours in the game. They are central because the limits on behaviour are often the key to the learning from the game. For example, a communication game may have a rule against talking—which may be the basis for learning the value of communication.

The learners must also know what they need to play the game. Some games don't require resources, others do. For those that need something other than the participants alone, you have to make it clear exactly what and where to find it. You don't want people breaking off halfway through a game because you didn't tell them they needed a prop, or a piece of flip chart paper. That break can cause all sorts of problems for your game.

Where you play the game can change its effectiveness—so make sure you tell people where you want them to play. For example, many games only work when there is space and people can physically spread out—if people try to play at their desks it can ruin the learning from the game.

It is only fair to tell people how long any activity will take and how it will end. By doing this you are also setting up completion at the right time and letting people know what they should be aiming for. If you don't do this you are liable to have a game that goes on forever.

We have already discussed the pitfall of overselling a game. If the game is difficult, be honest about it. You will only disillusion learners if you aren't, and break whatever trust you have already built.

> **What you have to include in the instructions:**
> 1 roles and rules
> 2 resources needed and where to find them
> 3 how long the game takes and how it ends
> 4 where to play it
> 5 a realistic view of any difficulties.

Short-circuit any reluctance and make people feel safe

When you get to give instructions it is important to comfort and reassure the learners that the situation is safe. You can do this by dropping back your own energy level, using a lower tone and keeping your gestures small. This change not only draws attention to you so you can give the instructions, it also allows you to withdraw later and let the learners lead the game after they understand the process.

In the same way you can address any issues or concerns that learners may show. These could include questions about their health, safety, and personal and emotional security. We looked at some suggestions for dealing with these in the pitfalls section.

When you are introducing the game it is important to monitor learner reactions to it. Pick out who's keen, who doesn't care and who seems stressed by the idea. Identify who may be negative about it. If they are a key opinion former for the group, you have to address their negativity. Even if they aren't, you need to be aware of it.

Once you have done all this and built a relationship around the game, there may still be people who don't want to play. You can give these people the option of not playing. This can be a dangerous step if you haven't monitored your audience closely. You should only give people this option when you think no-one will take it. If you think someone may opt out, it's an indicator that you haven't done the work explaining to and motivating the group. However, if someone does ask to opt out, let them. Offer them an observer role, make them your partner and keep them involved. If they simply wander off it excludes them and immediately drops the energy of the session.

You can also ask an open question for any reasons why you should not play the specific game suggested. This can get negativity out in the open without giving people the option of not playing.

Short-circuit any pitfalls

We looked at some common pitfalls of games earlier. In the introduction you can ensure that many of these do not occur. Open questioning about how people feel about the game can reveal if it's been done before, or if people have had bad experiences. Explaining clearly and motivating by values ensures it is relevant and has a point. By keeping the introduction brief you maintain interest and keep it fun. And by monitoring the response and enthusiasm of the audience you can tell whether they're going to be rowdy or flat.

Playing the game

Playing the game is the stage when you withdraw and let the learners get on with it. Apart from small clarifications, it is the time the learners do things on their own and you monitor their progress and take note of information to use in debriefing.

What you should do when playing the game
1 Let learners feel they can make decisions within the game.
2 Only intervene when necessary to keep the game going.
3 Stay out of the direct line of sight of learners.
4 Observe and monitor the players and the game.
5 Connect what you notice with how you want to debrief the game.
6 Run the game to help higher learning.
7 Take or allocate the overseer roles:
   * timekeeper
   * quality controller
   * issue collector
   * relevancy monitor.

The aim of playing the game is to allow learners to think, decide, act and learn for themselves. This allows them to invent, discover or steal information which makes their learning concrete and more effective. When playing a game it is your job to provide the ideal conditions for that to happen. To do this players have to:

* feel free to make their own decisions and be responsible for them
* feel that it's okay for them to make those decisions
* keep within the limits set by the rules
* be clear about what their role is and what they have to do.

Because of this, only intervene in the game when it is necessary. Let the learners find their own path to the game's outcome and their learning will be greater for it. Only when they are clearly bogged down and losing any benefit from the game is it the right time to intervene. If this happens, fix the problem and learn from the incident. Consider modifying your introduction for the next time you run the game to avoid the problem.

Step back from being the trainer

As the trainer you usually have no role within the game. However, you have to be there monitoring unobtrusively, noticing things, always understanding what happens, watching all groups at the same time. You have to do this at the same time as withdrawing from the sight of the learners. If you come into the learners' line of sight they are likely to ask you questions and try to drag you into their version of the game.

Stepping back means you assume the role of observer, not coach. If you act as a coach and jump in to correct each little mistake, you can stop learners discovering things for themselves. This is a question of balance—clearly you have to intervene if they are way off track or if emotional or practical issues require it. But where possible you should let participants be as autonomous as they can be.

One way to do this is to go to the back of the room. This makes it clear you are in a different role from that of trainer-in-charge. If you stay at the front you will still get questions. Don't drink coffee or relax yourself because this suggests the game is unimportant. Instead, move around the room to monitor the players.

Monitor the game and the players

Monitoring is essential. It allows you to tell when problems arise and to gather the information necessary to prepare a guided debrief. In the process, don't use a clipboard because this make players feel they are being examined and creates anxiety. Rather, you have to rely on your memory as you monitor and manage:

- players' energy level and task focus
- any confusion about what they have to do
- any unproductive behaviour such as personal criticism, allocating blame, interrupting or being self-centred
- any emotional or personal reaction (though this is unlikely unless you are running a personal development course)
- people who are not participating, who you might deal with by:
  - intervening politely
  - quietly drawing the attention of the group to them
  - negotiating to include them or make them an observer of the game.

At the same time as you note what you overhear, you can work out where and in what way to debrief the game. You can think about how to move from playing the game to finishing it, and from there to the debrief. You can also identify examples and behaviours to use in the debrief. For example, in a course on project management I saw several people whose interest waned toward the end of the game. I connected this lack of focus at the finish with the problems of not seeing a project through.

By asking targeted questions you can get the learners to volunteer the information you overheard. Why say it back to them when they can say it themselves?

Helping higher learning

When you run a game there are some things you can do so participants can more easily invent, discover and steal information:

- Keep all participants in the same room.
- Get groups to present back to the whole group rather than themselves (the individual game outcomes are less relevant than the stolen or discovered information created in the whole group).
- Ask guided questions about players overhearing something interesting.
- Ask guided questions about what the learners created.

The game overseer role

There are several roles that you have to fulfil to ensure the game is run properly. Usually you will do them all yourself. However, you don't necessarily have to. If the numbers aren't right, or individuals can't play for some other reason, you can allocate some of your functions to them. You can build into a game the same sort of roles for participants, such as:

- timekeeper. This can be useful when you start to run out of time and people want to keep playing. By having an allocated timekeeper you can refer to 'the rules'. In that way you avoid any criticism and maintain the relationship you've established.
- quality controller. A person can monitor the rate of progress of players, ensure that they get the set tasks finished, check the standards of what was done, and report on the quality of any part of the game.
- issue collector. A person can monitor the difficulties, arguments, discovered learning and cooperation of the game, and write up a check list for the trainer or group. This can help the debrief.
- relevancy role. This can be someone who monitors the debrief process for comments that wander off track, or for ways of connecting to the content from earlier sessions. It can streamline the debrief process, but has to be done by someone who is restrained and responsible.

The sting in the tail—Debriefing the game

The debrief is where the real learning takes place. Here you connect your training outcomes to what happened in the game and what people felt about the game. By the skilled use of questions and guided conversation, you can clarify the connections that learners have already made in playing the game.

This step is the most important in the game process. Most game failures are due to inadequate or unplanned debrief. When people play games that aren't debriefed, they rightly feel that the game is a waste of time. It is the debrief that creates the 'Ah-ha!' that makes the game worthwhile, and that makes the learning stronger. It allows you to assess the results of the game and to reinforce the main points of the content you've presented. By pushing the application of the game it allows the learners to extend it to other areas. And finally, it allows you to close the game and bring learners back to where they can cover more content.

All the benefits of games that I have mentioned rely on a successful debrief.

Steps in debriefing the game
1 Make the move from playing to debriefing.
2 Recall what happened during the game.
3 Ask guided questions about what the learners felt.
4 Ask guided questions to lead the learners to recognise the training outcome.
5 Invite learners to identify what they learnt and how it applies to the workplace.
6 Make the learning real by finding out what people will do with it.
7 Close the game and return to normal training.

Make the move from playing to debriefing

Learners have to distinguish the playing from the debriefing. This allows them to take a different perspective on the game and to learn from it. To help them do this, give them time to take it all in, chat with other participants and generally separate from the experience.

At the same time you have to make sure people stop playing their game roles. Make it clear it's time to stop and return to normal. Back this up by talking to people as you would normally, and going back into your leading trainer role.

Use the debrief environment to your advantage

The environment you debrief in can affect the sort of information the learners connect to the game. For example, if you return to desks to debrief, you take the learners out of the game and back to the place they encountered the content. This is too big a jump from the game, and people leave the application of the content behind in the game space. This is a *state change* that returns to the association with sitting and listening. Learners need to be in a place that allows them to make connections rather than be content-focused.

There are several ways you can do this. For example, you can leave the group standing to debrief. This connects to a different state and accelerates the debrief. It's useful if you want a quick, simple debrief. Another extreme may be to sit on the carpet when the group returns from playing. Clearly this depends on the type of training and the group, but it is a clear marker that you a doing something different. It's powerful when it works; people are happier to give more open commentary on the game and the debrief can last longer. But you have to be sure you can take the group with you. I've plonked down on the floor only to see everyone looking at me strangely! Only do what the relationship will bear.

Returning to the desks undermines a deep debrief. What it also does is cut short any waffling. If you need a short, sharp, not very profound debrief, going to desks can be useful.

The debrief environment is so important that once I spent 15 minutes during the game removing the desks and chairs for a two-minute debrief. As it happened, it was the end of a conference and people ended up singing a song together and really bonding as a team. That bonding couldn't have happened if I hadn't made the effort to make the debrief environment right.

Recall and present what you observed

The key to the debrief is to quickly get talking about learner responses and the *meaning* of what happened. For that reason, briefly summarise what happened and what you noticed during the game. Do it in general terms and keep up the tempo. This summary will give learners a framework to remember their own experiences. You'll key into those experiences and connect them with your learning outcomes later through guided questioning.

As part of the summary you can involve learners by asking what they noticed happening. At first you will get simple reports of the facts. You can then work with those facts when you start asking more pointed questions. Be aware that some learners may bombard you with details you don't need—so guide any answers towards the significant events. This is a way of leading into questions about the meaning of the game.

Now is also the time to start resolving any arguments about what happened. The most productive way of doing this once an argument is in the open is by asking questions. Ask them to think about why there is a disagreement. What was it about the game that caused it? How does it relate to everything else you looked at in the session? As a trainer you can use the disagreement to move on to the issue of the process of the game and the learning outcome.

Create guided questions and get the learners to volunteer information

As part of your preparation you will have created questions for debrief. These questions have to:

- ask what people experienced or felt during the game
- find out if the learners' discoveries match the learning outcome
- aim at getting a response that matches the learning outcome
- lead learners to see the outcome of the game
- get the learners to regurgitate some of the content they have met.

The key is to ask what people learnt or discovered from the game. This could be for the individual or for the group. When someone answers, they can be developing their own learning as they speak, so don't interrupt. Validate what they say and check if others feel that way.

Whenever you ask a question, always allow a little time for silence. People will usually fill a silence, so it can be a great incentive for someone to talk about the learning from the game. When there's silence, look interested in the learners and project a 'wise' and unthreatening feeling.

If that fails, look for someone who catches your eye—often this means they can answer but don't want to jump in. But ultimately, if no-one speaks up, you'll have to confront them about not answering.

If you want particular people to answer your directed questions, you don't have to name them. Rather, you can hold eye contact with them in an inviting, non-accusing manner, and talk about the question in general. That way you invite them to pipe up and say 'Yeah, I found that ...'. Getting people to repeat what you overheard shouldn't be confrontational or threatening for the learners.

Keep to the point

When you get a response from a learner that is about their experience, but leads you away from the learning outcome, it's easy to come back to the point. Firstly, agree with their comment, then say something else that's true, and then say something related to the outcome. In this way you link their point with the outcome by using the truth of something else you observe. For example:

> 'I can see that you could be angry about falling over John. Interrupting the game is annoying and falling over is a problem. Many people would probably respond in some similar way, and this really highlights how important communication/project management/etc really is ...'

The learner response doesn't 'highlight' anything. It only seems to follow because you've associated it with three true statements that went before.

Another way of getting back on track is to generalise from someone's experience to a broad category, then ask if others in the group have shared the broad category (not the specific experience of the learner). For example:

> 'Falling over John when you were playing must have been a problem. And it's a good example of the sorts of obstacles that can come up in anything you do. Can anyone give me an idea of the sort of obstacles they may encounter applying this anywhere else?'

Focus on the meaning of what happened, not what happened

When asking your guided questions, don't get bogged down in the details of what happened ('I fell over John'). Take people one step back from the game and focus more on the meaning they now make of what happened. It's in the area of meaning that they do their learning, so the more time you spend there the better. ('What did falling over John do to the game?' 'What does it mean in general?')

The 'So what?' question is important here. It asks people to take the step from what they did to what it meant. You can also ask questions—such as 'What next?', 'Why is that important?', 'Where does that take us?'—that extend the meaning. The idea is to reveal the learning for both now *and* other times and circumstances. The only way to do that is to distance people from the petty details.

Identify any unproductive behaviours and use them

When you monitor the game you may notice learners who are behaving inappropriately. You can draw this out in the debrief and discuss such behaviour, making people aware of it in the hope of change. It's important that the discussion stay general and that you avoid specific personal examples.

The sort of thing you may notice is personal criticism, allocating blame or point scoring for the fun of it. You can make good use of comments such as 'Why don't you just do it', 'You were the one in a hurry, not me', and 'If we'd done it slowly from the start ...'. If people interrupt too often, or speak only using 'I', it can indicate they think they are the leader, or that they aren't very good team players.

Bringing up these sorts of comments is a great debriefing tool that can open opportunities for personal change.

Connect to the introduction and the purpose of the session

In your introduction to the game you will have made the game relevant and meaningful. Learners view the game with this introduction in mind. At the end of the game, you have to give them the 'pay-off'. Either by asking questions or by showing them, lead them to see that they have done what you said they would. Remind them of how they started the game and how far they've come.

Connect the game firmly to the workplace

This step is often overlooked in games, and when it is overlooked the game is useless. To get any benefit from the game you have to lead the group to commit to change in the workplace.

The 'So what?' question applies here too. By forcing learners to take the next step, you get the extension of the learning that makes it more meaningful. Quite often one learner may ask you 'So what?' and another learner will volunteer the answer. When learners answer your guided questions, be willing to ask things like 'And what does that mean for you in the workplace?' or 'What can you take from that when you leave this room?'

It's important to link what people learn from the game to a specific time in the future when they will have applied it. Ask them to describe how work will be different when it has been applied and what will change. This sets up a challenge to their capabilities and a commitment to a vision of what change to make.

You can also link the learning from the game to new values you may have set up throughout the session. By linking to learner values, the outcome becomes more real and more important to the learner.

There are many ways to make this commitment. For example, you can:

- create a Change Action Plan as a group and tailor individual copies for each learner
- create Personal Action Plans that learners can take with them, or that you can post to them soon after the session to remind them of what they've learnt.

In any such action plan you can include a way to measure its success or to review it periodically.

> **What to remember in debriefing**
> 1 Give time for learners to change state before debriefing.
> 2 Use the debrief environment to your advantage.
> 3 Recall what happened in the game.
> 4 Ask guided questions and get the learners to volunteer what they felt and learned.
> 5 Keep to the point.
> 6 Focus on the meaning of what happened, not what happened.
> 7 Identify any unproductive behaviours and use them to your own ends.
> 8 Connect to the introduction and purpose of the session.
> 9 Connect the game firmly to the workplace.

A participant-centred dialogue model

This is an example debrief of a hypothetical game focusing on communication.

Trainer	Participant
Can you give me an example of when you didn't understand each other?	
	When we stood together talking about lunch.
How did that affect the team?	
	We were totally confused and getting nowhere with the problem.
And what did you do to respond to the situation?	
	One of us took charge and made sure we brainstormed ways of moving forward.
How did you feel when this happened?	
	I was a little upset at first, but it worked really well, and I can see it was the right thing to do.
Why did it upset you?	
	Well, as usual, no-one asked me about it.
When you think about communication, what do you get out of all this?	
	Well, we need it to get the project done. And it would have been nice if we'd had some before Mark took charge.
So does this relate to your work at all?	
	Yeah. Day-to-day if we don't communicate we have the same problems. And everyone gets annoyed when management just does things without telling us.
So what sort of changes could help?	
	More timely explanations from management and consensus about our direction, and more discussion of day-to-day problems. We need a daily team brief.
What can you do?	
	I can give more feedback, and listen more to what others are saying is happening.

Managing groups

Many games involve dividing the learners into groups. If you have skills at creating and managing these groups, running games will be a lot easier. You will also be able to deal with specific problems by regrouping people in a controlled way.

Who should go in a group?

The type and make up of your groups depends on your game. But if the game doesn't require any particular group set-up, aim to have:

- a good gender mix in all groups
- even rather than odd numbers of people in each group
- one extrovert in every group
- a rotation through groups throughout the day.

People tend to group themselves by gender, even though some people prefer to be in the minority. Real life is a mix of genders and this should be reflected in your games. This is important because the game, and the group, is a way of making the training concrete and connected to the real world.

Some trainers have reported that groups with even numbers have less internal conflict than those with odd numbers. The reasons behind this haven't been clarified, but I suspect that in odd-numbered groups there is more alliance-making and exclusion than in even-numbered ones.

Extroverts are people who gain their energy from being with people. They're outgoing, they initiate conversation, they animate groups. This sort of person can act as a group's internal icebreaker and get things moving.

If learners get too settled in a group, they slip into a comfort zone where it is difficult to lead them to break their habits. Because of this you need to change the make-up of groups throughout the day. I look at how to do this subtly in the section on counting off.

How many should be in a group?

The size of the groups you use clearly depends on the total group size and the type of game you want to play. There are, however, a few clear guidelines on group sizes:

- keep groups to less than seven people—any more than that and you lose the value of grouping
- if you are on your own, keep the total group number under 20—any more than this and you'll need administrative support to make sure people follow instructions.

Groups at the start

The larger the number of people in the room, the more detailed you have to be with your instructions. For big groups, write up the instruction steps. For very big groups follow them up with a handout from support staff.

You don't always need a big 'Get-to-know-you' opening game. Some of them are so clichéd that all they do is bring up memories of bad training sessions. The game or the counting-off method can function just as well in familiarising people. And you don't have to introduce everyone in the group—you can let them introduce themselves. This is quite easy if they have name tags.

Having said that, some games are very useful as openers. As with much in training, it's up to your judgement when a game is appropriate and when it will contribute to your outcome.

Ways of counting off to get the groups you want

There are many ways of manipulating who goes in each group. You may need to do this to ensure a mix of genders, or introverts and extroverts, or to break up a group that has proven rowdy in earlier sessions. Where possible you should do this unobtrusively—breaking up groups that have already chosen themselves implies that you aren't happy with the people in that group. The easiest way of doing this unobtrusively is by using different counting methods.

Counting methods allocate people to certain groups on different bases. You should always have several counting methods as options so you can create the groups you want. These are three examples of methods I use:

- coloured name tags
- places on a line
- counting off with numbers.

The only way to change groups effectively is to take control with a counting method. Don't try to change groups by asking people to group with someone they haven't worked with before. People won't listen, because there is no incentive for them to break with previously established relationships.

It can be a good idea to put up signs for people to group under before you start at the beginning of the day. You can have sheets with colours and mixes of colours around the walls, or large numbers. These designate meeting spots for the different groups you may count off. This can generate some positive curiosity. It also helps because it gets people to move and change state when they go into groups.

Coloured name tags: At the beginning of the day I give out name tags to every participant. Those name tags are broken up into equal numbers of different colours. Throughout the day I can make groups:

- of the same colour
- with everyone a different colour
- with certain combinations of colours (for example, 'Make sure you have two greens or two blues in your group').

The benefit of this is that the method is set up from the beginning, and it is easy to remember that the all-green group is a rowdy one you don't want together again. It also focuses people on the name tags and the names, and helps develop learner relationships.

Places on a line: You can get the learners to line up on the basis of some quality that moves up in steps. It could be height, years in the business, age, first initial or whatever. Then you can put every second person in one group, every third in another and so on.

As with the coloured name tags, it is important to have good forward vision and to work out what sort of groups you are likely to make before you start counting. It is also important to choose a quality that won't be embarrassing for people to admit to. Once I made a line based on the amount of hair people had. It seemed simple enough, but for those men starting to lose their hair it was a sensitive issue. Strangely enough, the bald men had no problem with it, and were quite proud to be at the head of the line.

This is also a great combination of an introduction and a count-off method. In negotiating their place on the line, learners interact and develop relationships. By introducing and grouping people in one step, it is a more seductive way of building group rapport.

Count off with numbers: This is a simple count off. You walk around the room, allocating people to groups 1, 2, 3 and so on. This is the method most people are familiar with, but it can prove difficult to generate new groups in a simple way if people remain in the same seats. You can start counting in different places, but the level of control over who goes in which group is a lot less.

Another Magnificent Seven: Rules for managing games
1 Brief participants on the game.
   • Ensure they understand the game is relevant.
   • Don't give them more information than they need to see the game is relevant.
   • Generate positive feeling through fun and your presentation.
2 Explain the rules of the game.
3 Explain what each person has to do.
4 Establish the appropriate setting and environment for the game.
5 Let the game run with minimum interference.
6 Take note of what happens as the game progresses.
7 Debrief thoroughly what happened, what people felt and how the game relates to the workplace.

The games environment

Where you play and debrief can make or break your game. First, it can help to change state, which helps the game work. Second, if the environment makes the game difficult to play, it discourages learners from playing. To start with, many learners feel safer to sit and passively absorb a lecture at a desk. If the environment doesn't suit, it just gives learners another reason to reject the game.

Learners won't go into a game-playing mode if they're in a confined space or buried behind desks, because these are the wrong environments. And if you use the same environment to lecture, play and debrief, you run the risk of associating one mode of learning with another and losing the value of the game. For all these reasons you have to ensure the environment will work with your game.

Most rooms are not set up for games. To overcome this you have to inspect the environment before running the session. That is the only way you'll know if the room can handle the games you've planned.

As we saw in running a game, you have to provide:

• space, to minimise distractions and stop groups from being on top of each other
• the right number of tools and props
• the right music during the game to keep energy up, particularly if the game goes for more than 10 minutes
• a game space *in* the training room, to keep learners focused and familiar with the instructions.

In an ideal world, we would train and play our games in the workplace. This would, among other things, allow for a very strong connection of the training content to the real world. Sadly, this never happens, and for very good practical reasons.

The next best circumstance would be a room three times the size of the classic training room. This way you can physically separate content areas from game and from debrief, all without leaving the training space. A folding door opening onto another training room would be good enough.

This gives you the ability to put groups in the corners of the room, far enough apart to not distract each other. When you place those groups, setting up the chairs for the group can set its tone. Always try to have an even setting of chairs so that no-one is excluded.

Actually leaving the training room to go to another games room is a poor solution. By leaving the room there is a lessening of focus and the chance of more distractions. And for some reason people lose track of game instructions once they leave the training room.

Managing problem participants

Problem participants pop up in two places: at the start of the game and during it. A good introduction embraces such participants and counters their early objections. However, during the game different types of problems arise when people:

- are defensive due to insecurity
- isolate themselves
- talk too much
- act like a know-all
- rescue others and forget their own playing
- wander about the training room
- clash with others.

Steps in managing problem participants
1 Work out what's happening before you act.
2 Work out why people are acting as they are.
3 Take a step back from the situation and your own feelings.
4 Work out a win-win solution, where people can continue to play but still have their feelings validated.
5 Create an alternative solution in case you need it.
6 Rehearse your delivery if you have a chance.
7 Intervene with the participant.
8 Offer an insistent participant an observer's or other role in the game.

Different types of learners

It may seem obvious, but you have to remember that people are different, and that what you see as a problem may be because someone approaches the world in a different way. There are all sorts of learning styles, values and ways of thinking that can affect how people approach games.

This is where the first three steps of this process are important. When you take your time to understand what is going on and step outside your own perspective, you can enter the learners' world. There you can begin to see the sorts of values and styles that cause the responses you see, which will enable you to create appropriate interventions.

There are entire books on value types and learning styles, so I won't go into the details here. But the sort of preferences you need to look out for include:

- learning styles based on seeing, hearing or doing things
- learning with people or alone
- learning by following a procedure or by finding their own way
- active or passive learning
- theoretical or practical learning.

These sorts of preferences can push someone away from games. For example, someone who prefers to meet theory on their own before doing anything else may not like to play games.

In general, you can overcome these differences with an adequate introduction to the game. Sometimes, however, when you are playing the game particular problems come up that you have to deal with separately.

How to handle different problem participants

These are a few suggestions for dealing with specific problem participants. It's a good idea to try the more subtle steps first. However, when someone is causing a problem in a game and they don't respond, your last option is always to confront them privately and let them know their behaviour is inappropriate. Your responsibility is to the entire training audience, and you have to be willing to confront one person if that allows the remainder to get the training they deserve.

It should only rarely come to that point. Most people are considerate and will respond to the other steps you take.

Defensive

A person becomes defensive when they feel that their value as a person is under attack. This is a normal response to this type of feeling and is aimed at protecting how people see themselves. For example, I may become defensive when someone asks me to do something I know I should have done. I act to defend myself from what I think will be criticism of me.

With this sort of participant, the first thing to do is lend your support and provide lots of encouragement. Be empathetic and understanding. It could be fear of failure, or fear of criticism that the learner is feeling. To overcome this, try breaking the tasks down into smaller chunks, so they appear less daunting. Give the learner a chance to have some small 'wins' so they can gain confidence. You can also build confidence by reminding learners of successes they have already achieved.

Isolated and silent

Some learners withdraw, want to be left alone and will not offer information. They may respond to questions with one-word answers. If you ask them directly what the problem is, they may not tell you, or play dumb and claim they don't know. This can have the same causes as defensiveness, or it could be due to intense introversion or shyness.

There are two things to do. Firstly, you must build the relationship you have with the learner, and try to strengthen their relationships within the group. Drop your own energy level and speak softly to them. Include them in discussions you have with others. Try to place them with other introverts. If they are with extroverts they will stay quiet and allow themselves to be dominated. Keep them close to you and monitor for when they want to speak.

Secondly, keep challenging their isolation. Ask them open questions they can't answer in one word. Keep your expression open and keep waiting for an answer. Don't be put off by awkward silences and don't jump in to relieve the pressure.

If you are training one-on-one, don't let them escape. Set an appointment to resume the session and follow up.

Talk too much

Learners can talk too much. One person can dominate or distract learners by monopolising the discussion or going off the point. Often this is motivated by a desire to impress. Sometimes, when these people feel they have made an impression, they begin to quieten down. Therefore, as your first response, validate their comment and thank them for it.

If they keep talking, ask them to back up their claims with reasons. When they do, open the discussion to the group. If it remains a problem, try to redirect their energy to help out the group, by giving them helping tasks. You can also take them aside at breaks, acknowledge their contribution, and suggest that some of the other learners may need more help. Flatter them by asking them to quieten down so you can help some slower learners.

Act like a know-all

Learners who are subject-matter experts, or who have a head start on the other learners, can sometimes try to dominate the session. They may act as though they know everything on the topic and be condescending to other learners.

This is similar to the very talkative learner. They are probably motivated by a need to impress. However, they are a bit harder to manage, especially if they know their stuff.

Get your facts together. You can't afford to be proven to be wrong, because it will undermine your training credibility. If you have to disagree, do so in a friendly and respectful manner. Treat the person's knowledge as interesting. Make counterpoints by asking questions or by agreeing first then moving to a related idea. For example, your response could be 'Yes, I can see that communication is often irrelevant, and I can also see that in some cases ...'. Avoid using 'but' when you respond—it has a sense of contradiction that you can avoid by using 'and'.

Find a way to let them take a bow. If appropriate, give them public credit for their knowledge. If not, give them private credit even if they don't know what they're talking about. Stroking their ego may settle them down.

As we did for the talkers, you can also distract them by getting them to do tasks for the group.

Rescue others and forget their own playing

A learner governed by good intentions will apologise, defend, explain and interpret unnecessarily for others. This behaviour interferes with the learning other people can get from the game.

Take them aside and recognise their good intentions. Make them feel you appreciate their efforts and that they have done something good. But move on to say that it is important for people to speak for themselves in order to learn. Explain it is the only way you can train without misunderstandings. Treat them as an equal who is concerned about the other learners. Support this by getting them to do tasks for the group.

Wander about the training room

During the game people can wander about, interrupting others and interrupting you. This is a danger sign that there is something wrong with the session or the game, so review closely what is happening before you intervene. When you are sure that it isn't a fundamental problem of the session, politely explain the problem. Be firm. Explain that there is only a set time for the game, that it is central to the day and so on. If they don't want to play, offer them an observer or overseer role.

Clash with others

When there is a real clash of personalities you must act quickly. This may come about when you have two of the problem participants we have already spoken about. For example, two know-alls in one group are bound to clash.

Deal with the matter by focusing on the points made by each party. Remind people that differences of opinion are healthy and constructive. Identify any common ground and build on it. Keep your own opinion out of it.

You can take some heat out of any situation by taking it to the group in general. After discussing it, try to connect the conflicting ideas with the training outcome and return to the game.

You may want to separate the pair if they are in a small group. Only do so after you have resolved the clash, and use a counting method to do it unobtrusively.

If a conflict continues after the end of the game, talk with the learners privately and insist that the conflict be dealt with out of the class.

Stay safe—Keeping games under control

Some learners may have had a bad experience with a game and may feel threatened by the prospect of other games. Learners may be shy or stammer or have some sort of disability that makes game playing difficult. Provided you have prepared both the relationship and the game well enough, these shouldn't be problems for you. You may remember the things we have talked about already:

- investigate your learners' backgrounds as much as possible
- get to know your learners and monitor their reactions
- build a relationship with them and use fun to make games seem safe
- keep games reasonably short to retain interest and enthusiasm
- make sure they see that the game is relevant
- be aware that music can be emotionally powerful
- use observer roles for those unable to play.

Even if you do this occasionally learners may still feel threatened. Always give people who seem threatened the option to play or to sit out as an observer. If there are large numbers of people who want to sit out, it indicates that you haven't established a strong enough relationship with the group to play the game, and that a game would be inappropriate anyway.

Humour is an important tool for safety. It short-circuits any over-intense emotional investment in a game—you can use fun to get people ready to play a game, even if they would never play under normal circumstances.

The likelihood of people finding emotional issues coming up is far less than some people may suggest. Some trainers treat learners like fragile flowers, whose emotions are constantly ready to overflow in an uncontrollable way. Or treat them in a way that holds that only their emotional responses govern their behaviour. My belief is that games in training do not have a likelihood of opening emotional issues unless you as a trainer invite them in. If you introduce a game and say 'Be prepared for this game to bring up emotional issues for you' then you invite emotional reactions. If you don't open the door to them, if you build the relationship and make the game relevant, emotional issues are very unlikely to appear.

The exception to this is in intimate personal development training. Here the subject matter is enough to create an emotional response, regardless of the role of the game. But these issues are not present in most training rooms and the emotional response they generate won't be either.

Occasionally people can get over-competitive in games. People who are sedate and non-competitive can get angry at those who are highly competitive. Competitive people can be socially inappropriate when they are wrapped up in the game. It's important to keep an eye on these things but they don't pose a problem in themselves. In fact, it is constructive to debrief on these sorts of different responses to the game—it is one of the strengths of games to have varied responses to debrief. This sort of conflict is good for the game and the session. Besides, conflict is so general that you can link it to any topic that you are presenting.

Designing your own games

Being able to design games is a useful skill for trainers and is no more complicated than designing a training session. The principles are similar and the results are remarkable. Having design skills will allow you to create on-the-spot games when you need them and to tailor games to particular audience needs. This is the sort of difference in skill that makes a trainer truly outstanding.

> **Steps in designing games**
> 1 Ensure there is a valid training need.
> 2 Work out if a game is a good intervention to meet that need.
> 3 Create the game.
> 4 Confirm the game meets the training need.
> 5 Test the game.
> 6 Use the game.
> 7 Enhance the game based on experience.

The training need and the game

A normal training needs analysis will identify a performance problem or a development need. When you have a valid training need and you've designed a program, you are in a position to work out if a game is a good tool to use.

How to work out if you want to use a game

At first you have to look at the topic you are dealing with, whether the game fits the timing of your session and if your audience is suitable for learning through games. You should have already gathered this sort of information in your training needs analysis, or for your program design. I mentioned earlier that some topics don't really suit game-style learning, and that some audiences, particularly senior ones, don't like games at all. These sorts of issues are something you have to investigate for each training situation.

When you look at the topic and timing of your program, you need to ask yourself if you want to achieve any of the things games can achieve:

- Put learners in the right place to learn.
- Make the learning concrete.
- Make a bridge between knowledge and action.
- Help learners reach a higher-level learning.
- Produce creative solutions.
- Allow monitoring of learning.
- Change pace and energy.

If you want to gain one or more of these benefits at that stage in your program, then a game is a good way to do it.

Work out what you want to achieve with the game

When you are committed to using a game, the key is to identify what you want to achieve with the game and to express it in clear terms. All this takes place before you have any idea of what the game looks like. It's important that you express it clearly because it is the guide for your game design.

For example, let's say I have just completed a long theory session on influence skills. After analysing my program and audience, I feel I need something to spark energy in people and to make the content of the course concrete. A game would work well.

Create a new game

When you've established all the preliminaries—the need and purpose of the game, and the nature of the audience—you actually have to come up with a game. This is the part many people find difficult. But creating a game isn't a mystical skill and doesn't require a magnificent imagination. All you have to do is follow a simple procedure and you'll come up with a reasonable game. Of course the more creative you are the better the game will be—but you can still create games that will work well without amazing creativity.

> **Coming up with a new game**
> 1 Work out what family of game you want to use.
> 2 Brainstorm the players' goal for the game.
> 3 Let yourself go wild with filling out the details of the game.

Families of games

It can help you create new games if you understand some of the categories of games you can draw on. By being familiar with these game types you'll have more conscious choice when you try to create one. These categories are overlapping and incomplete—but they give a guide to the types of games available that you can add to as you gain more experience.

Game family	Examples (general and in this book)
Card	Poker, Euchre, Snap, Pass the Deck, Dealing with Know-Alls
Board	Monopoly, Snakes and Ladders, Ludo
Word/Communication	Taboo, Articulate, Charades, Anagrams, Are You Listening, Walkies, Fists
Build/create	House of Cards, storytelling, Build a Paper Plane, The Opera House
Memory	Trivia, What Can You Remember, Change Game
Mental challenge/puzzle	Crosswords, Rubik's Cube, Anagrams, What Can You Remember, Mish-Maths
Physical challenge/knack	Pick-up-sticks, arm wrestle, dances, poses, Apple and Straw Game, Walkies
Roles and mime	Charades, acting games, The Feast
Ball	Catch
Sound and listening	Pick the Sound, End with a Bang

Key elements in the new game

When you design the game you have to work out the:

- goal of the game (this is what the players aim for, not the training outcome)
- game challenges or obstacles
- roles and rules

- time limits
- element of fun
- props, materials, space and numbers required
- way the game ends.

The key to creating the game is the goal. Once you know the type of game you need and the goal players have to reach, you can play with ways to make it more or less difficult, how fast it is, what challenges players face and how it can be more fun. To make these variations you simply play with the elements that make up the game—those things listed above and explained earlier in this section.

Worked example of creating a game—influence skills

Let's continue our example of a game to illustrate influence skill theory. My schedule is such that I only have 20 minutes at most to get the game played and debriefed. I'd like the game to make the content on influence skills concrete, and give people a change of state to improve their energy levels.

The following questions that I ask are a guide to what you should ask yourself when you are creating a game.

What family of game would be easiest to relate to influence skills?

Probably it would need to be a word or communication game that might involve roles, where people can try to influence and others can resist. Or it could involve a physical challenge where something resists what the players are trying to do, which I can explain as a metaphor for influence and resistance. But because a word or communication game makes a more direct link to influence, I'll stick with that type of game.

What goal would be appropriate to make my content concrete and to fit in with the type of game I want?

It's here you can indulge your creativity and come up with wild ideas. You'll reject most of them. But in the process you'll surely come up with a good idea. Here's a list of a few I came up with off the top of my head:

- getting a group to do what you want without using words
- persuading a partner to do something by using preset words and body language
- getting a partner to hand over money without giving a guarantee to give it back
- getting someone to open a fist
- have everyone except one person in the group do the same thing until that one person conforms
- collecting enough water to survive (for example, a cup) when there are only two-cup jugs of water available, and not enough for everyone
- convincing the Queen to be a republican.

This list isn't that inspiring—but regardless there are several ideas you could make into a game. You may notice that I have already—the game Fists is about communicating to get someone to open a fist. For this example, let's say the goal is to convince a partner to hand over money without giving a guarantee to give it back. This goal is the general framework around which you can fiddle to make your game work.

How can I fill out the game?

Once you have a goal that the players can work towards, you can start thinking about the details, and the sorts of elements we've looked at. For example, we can make our game competitive by awarding a prize to the person who gets the most money from their partner. We apply a time limit of 10 minutes to fit our timeslot and allow for debrief. We can add random obstacles to the process by giving the partners secret instructions—saying they must refuse to hand over money until the influencer uses a certain word or does a certain thing. And there already is a major obstacle in the game—not giving a guarantee of returning the money.

Your creativity can run wild when it comes to adding fun to the structure of the game. You can allocate roles to people, asking them to pretend to be John Elliot or Alan Bond. You can put up a $5 prize for the most outrageous argument or creative performance. At the end of the game you can ask those who got money to go to the 'Wall Street' corner of the room and those who didn't to go to the 'Shantytown' corner.

I came up with this simple game as I was writing this section. It's not a great game, and because it involves money I probably wouldn't use it. But it took me all of five minutes to create it from scratch. It's that easy.

Sources of ideas for new games

But you don't have to rely solely on yourself for ideas and creativity. If you keep your eyes peeled for new ideas, you'll find many ways to get ideas for new games. The simplest source of inspiration is to play as many games as possible. I have friends who have games groups, who regularly get together to try out new board, paper, acting and card games—just for fun. Always keep your trainer's hat on, and your eye out for good ideas. Often you can adapt an old idea to something perfect for your training.

You can expand on this by visiting toy stores, watching game shows and children's programs on TV, and reading books on training games. Visit adult games stores, and make time to play with kids.

You can also convert ordinary exercises into games by adding an element of fun, competition or cooperation. The exercise already focuses on the learning outcome, so if you can spice it up, it's ready-made as a game.

Use networking and modelling to discover tried and tested games. Training is a practical field and you can learn a lot from others' experiences. Join industry organisations and pursue further education in training and presenting. These are all opportunities to gather information on games and on training in general.

However, it is still important to reverse your engineering. Don't focus solely on finding a great game. Remember that you have to create a game to match a particular learning. Games on their own are pretty much useless until you match them with a learning outcome.

Test the game and confirm it meets the training need

Never overlook testing. Once you have a prototype game, test it into the ground before you use it in a session. Let other trainers look at it, run pilots to friends and workmates, and review it based on the feedback you get.

Testing provides the information you need to make your games a success. It is essential preparation for any successful trainer. Testing is also an opportunity to confirm that you've stayed on track. Always check that the game actually meets the training need you started from. In our example case, that was to create a change of pace and to make influence skills theory more concrete.

When you finally get a chance to run the game, observe it even more closely than usual. Take notes, think about variations and ask the learners what they think. They can come up with great improvements. Always be ready to enhance the model.

Design check list

☐ Topic, timing and audience all suitable for a game?

☐ Game contributes to what you want to achieve?

☐ Game learning outcome identified and written down?

☐ Does the time match the learning involved?

☐ Have you chosen a clear goal for players to aim at?

☐ Have you considered the option of observers?

☐ Have you provided time for explaining the game?

☐ Do you have a total time for the game and the debrief?

☐ Have you listed all preparation, props and aids you need to play the game?

☐ Have you brainstormed for possible mistakes and problems for players? Your solutions to those problems?

☐ Have you had a test run?

☐ Does the game conform to the original training objective? To the original game objective?

☐ Does the game produce an Ah-ha! response?

Part II
Guidelines to 50 great games

Before you play the games

Play every game according to the general principles

For each of the following games there is a summary of what is involved in preparing and playing them. The principles we looked at in the first section of this book—about preparation, introduction, conduct and debrief of games—apply to every game. Whenever you run one of these games, keep in mind the steps and the responses to problems that we have already looked at.

What I cover in each game

In many of the games I set out:

- Why it works for me
- Where it works best
- What you have to do
- What you have to look out for
- Debrief, including key debrief idea and sample debrief questions
- Variations

For some games I leave out some of these sections because they aren't relevant or because they simply repeat what I've written elsewhere. The most important sections are *What you have to do* and *Debrief*. In *What you have to do* I set out what you have to prepare and how to play the game. In *Debrief* I explain the key debrief idea and give some sample questions you can use to get a guided debrief going and get the most out of the game.

You can see how each game is laid out in the sample game on page 51.

Notes on *What to look out for*

In all the games there are certain things you have to watch for. These could be the pitfalls of the games we looked at in the previous section, or other problems we've already highlighted. On the other hand, they could be useful information or great examples.

It's often a good idea to skim the earlier sections of this book before you start a session—just to keep possible problems and responses in mind. As a reminder, you should always be looking for:

- people who refuse to participate, do so grudgingly or sabotage the game
- large numbers of people looking bored or disengaged
- raised voices or extreme quiet
- any overly emotional reactions.

If you encounter any of these sorts of problems you can deal with them in ways I discussed in the previous section. The important step is to address the problem, and to do so in a way that respects the participants' point of view. You generally have a choice of intervening immediately, taking note and monitoring, or leaving it to raise in debrief. As the trainer, you have to rely on your judgement of the situation.

As you play you should also be looking for useful and positive information you can use, both for the current training session and for future sessions. To help run the current game more effectively keep an eye out for:

- good quotes to use in debrief
- particular participants who had interesting problems or solutions to draw on in debrief
- creative interpretations of rules or problems

- opportunities to build more rapport with the participants and get to know individuals
- unexpected happenings that you can turn into a learning opportunity.

All these things appear as the participants are playing the game. Successful trainers are the ones that can use this information to its fullest advantage.

As that successful trainer, you'll always be learning from the people you train. Use each game as an opportunity to practise and perfect it, and to gain ideas for new games and variations. The more observant you are in each game, the more creative you can be in the future.

Notes on *Debrief*

We looked at the general principles underlying debrief in Part I, and these general principles apply equally to all the games that follow. But I have also given you some more specific help with debrief. For each game I have provided sample debrief questions, questions that have worked when I've tried to move a group towards a game's learning objectives.

These sample questions follow a pattern. In general, I'd advise you to follow a similar pattern with any debrief questions you choose to use. Structure the flow of your questions so that you:

- start with open, neutral questions that allow people to talk about their experience of the game
- allow people to talk freely about any roles they played
- work towards more open questions that will lead participants to your learning outcome
- remove participants' generalisations, distortions and avoidance of responsibility (fluff-bust)
- get participants to suggest the conclusions that they can take from the game.

I recommend this structure because people need room to express their initial responses to their experience. If they don't, their desire to express them will get in the way of addressing the learning outcome. You have to release the emotion of the game experience before you can take participants that one step further.

It is also important to allow people to volunteer their answers to your questions. Don't pick people out unnecessarily; if you do, be as sure as you can that they will be able to answer the question.

Notes on *Variations*

I've provided many ways that you can take these games and apply them to different situations. Generally I have given you specific steps to create a variation on a game. However, for every game in this book there are several general principles you can use to create variations. You can change the:

- time—vary how fast people play the game, or impose an unrealistic time limit
- competitive element—make the game competitive or non-competitive
- number of roles
- size of groups
- debrief—change the direction of the debrief to relate the game to other topics
- role or number of observers—include, exclude and change the function of observers.

Even with this limited scope you can still create games tailored to a specific learning situation. When you add your own creativity to the general structure of the game, the applications of even the most basic game are endless.

Have fun!

What's in each game

Time required to play	Number of participants required	Game subject

Why it works for me

A brief explanation of how and why this game has really worked for me in the past ... and why it has become one of my favourites.

Where it works best

The context in which I have discovered this game really takes off.

What you have to do

A list of instructions to help you to bring this game to life. I have left a space at the end of this section to enable you to add any additional instructions that you discover make the game even better as you practise it over time.

✏ WRITING SPACE

What to look out for

Things that I have discovered can side-track or ruin the game if you, as the trainer, are not watchful. Once again, take advantage of the space left for your personal notes.

✏ WRITING SPACE

Debrief

Key debrief idea

The most important issue or issues that you will try to make real for your game players within the context of the debrief.

Sample debrief questions

Some sample questions that I have used successfully with this game to generate discussion towards achieving the objectives of the debrief. Once again, take advantage of the space provided to document your own questions that you discover work well for the game debrief.

✏ WRITING SPACE

Variations

Some suggestions as to how you might create a new game by varying the game described.

The Future Space Game

15 minutes	20 maximum	Opener

Why it works for me

A good activity to get people talking, to find out what they need to know and expect from the course, and versatile enough to use for anything that involves planning or the future.

What you have to do

1 Get the participants to form a circle.

2 Tell them there is an invisible genie bottle on the floor at the centre of the circle. It has the power to grant any wish.

3 Ask a volunteer to start off the wishes by asking for something specific or abstract they want from the course. For example, knowledge, skills, attitudes, keeping the boss happy and so on.

4 Continue round the circle until everyone has a turn. Allow people to repeat wishes if they want.

5 Put the wishes on a flip chart and revisit them at the end of the course.

✏

✏

✏

Variations

Use it with any session that involves some future focus or some change in the future. For example, after a session on planning, on strategy, on attitude change and so on.

The Me Square

30 minutes	Any number	Opener

Why it works for me

A quick variation on opener games that allows people to say something positive and interesting rather than the usual boring introductions.

What you have to do

1 Prepare a 15-cm-square piece of paper and a pin for each participant.

2 Distribute the paper and pins.

3 Ask them to write their name in the centre of the paper.

4 Ask them to write:

- the name of someone they admire in the top left corner
- their favourite pastime in the bottom left corner
- the completed sentence 'The best thing about me is …' in the top right corner
- their greatest achievement in the bottom right corner.

5 Ask participants to pin on their tags and mingle. They should read and discuss what is on the tags and ensure they meet everyone in the room.

What to look out for

People who can't say anything good about themselves.

Debrief

Sample debrief questions

- What was the most interesting pastime or achievement you noticed?
- Who was the most interesting admired person?
- What did you learn about the range of people and ideas in the room?

Variations

You can use the idea of the square for any topic to get people's opinions and personalities into play. For example, write issues about the corporation on the card.

Who's That?

25 minutes	Any number	Opener

What you have to do

1 Prepare copies for each participant of the Who's That sheet (see following page).

2 Get the participants to form pairs.

3 Give each person a copy of the Who's That sheet.

4 Ask each person to ask the questions on the sheet of their partner, writing their responses on the sheet.

5 When all responses are recorded, have all participants introduce each other to the group, relying on their partner's responses from the sheet.

✎

✎

✎

What to look out for

• Taking too long to get the answers—keep the pace up.
• People who read the answers monotonously.

✎

✎

✎

Debrief

Sample debrief questions

• What was the most interesting desire or achievement you noticed?
• What was the most interesting thing people wanted to be described as?
• What did you learn about the range of people and ideas in the room?

✎

✎

✎

Variations

You can use this method to discover people's opinions and attitudes as well, particularly when they may not want to reveal them themselves.

Who's That sheet

Their middle name

. . . .

Where they work

. . . .

Have they ever been sacked?

. . . .

Two words that they would most like to be thought of as

. . . .

. . . .

Two words that they would least like to be thought of as

. . . .

. . . .

'When I grow up, I'd like to …'

. . . .

. . . .

. . . .

. . . .

Their proudest moment or achievement

. . . .

. . . .

. . . .

. . . .

Meet My Best Friend

25 minutes	Any number	Opener

Why it works for me

A quick variation on opener games that allows people to say something positive and interesting and that gets people talking about themselves in public.

What you have to do

1 Prepare copies of the Meet My Best Friend worksheet (see following page).

2 Ask the participants to complete the sheets as though they are their own best friend.

3 Arrange the participants in a single circle.

4 Go around the circle, having each person introduce themselves from the completed sheet. As they do this, each person must stand behind their chair and adopt the role of their best friend.

✏️

✏️

✏️

Debrief

Sample debrief questions

- How did you feel about the activity?
- Is it always hard to say something good about yourself?
- How difficult is it to move out of your comfort zone around that? Or around public speaking?
- Is it important to move out of your comfort zone? Why?

✏️

✏️

✏️

Meet My Best Friend worksheet

My best friend is …

....

S/he is my best friend because …

....

....

....

S/he is very good at …

....

....

....

I like the way s/he …

....

....

....

Sometimes s/he gets angry about …

....

....

....

S/he hopes that one day s/he will …

....

....

....

Who's Who Game

10 minutes	Any number	Opener/Workplace difference

Why it works for me

Versatile game that creates laughter with surprising answers. It's a safe way for participants to reveal something of themselves without making it too serious or therapy-like.

Where it works best

Participants must know each other at least a little—works in a divisional training or a midsize company for a opener game, or as a team-building game well into a session.

What you have to do

1 Prepare pieces of card large enough to write a sentence on.

2 Distribute the cards.

3 Ask the participants to think of something that is true of them and that only they know about. The fact may relate to the past or present. For example, 'I used to be in the Brownies' or 'I worked in a circus'.

4 Ask them to write this on the card in such a way that people won't recognise their handwriting (perhaps using their 'wrong' hand).

5 Collect the cards and display them on a table or wall so all participants can get a good look.

6 Gather the participants and have them guess who's who.

✏️

✏️

✏️

What to look out for

People who may want to retract what they write when they find it will be displayed—always let them change it if they insist.

✏️

✏️

✏️

Debrief

Sample debrief questions

- What was the most surprising thing? Why?
- Did you see things you expected? Why?
- What does this tell you about the people you thought you knew?
- What does it tell you about the people you work with?
- What resources might be available in the workplace that you didn't know about?

✎

✎

✎

Variations

It can apply to what they've done, something they own, someone famous they know and so on.

Dealing with Know-Alls

20 minutes	15	Openers

Why it works for me

A memory game that highlights the need for training. Perfect for those times you stand in front of a group and can see people thinking, 'Here we go again, another bloody trainer'. You can link this to a training need that people may not know they have.

Where it works best

Groups that are a bit suspicious of the value of the training you are about to present. Also works well when know-alls cause problems during a session.

What you have to do

1 Make sure you have a deck of cards with traditional face cards.

2 Display the cards on a table.

3 Explain, in a tongue-in-cheek way, that the participants have four minutes to look at every card, and then answer some questions.

4 After four minutes, ask them:

- How many kings wear moustaches?
- How many kings face right?
- How many kings don't carry a battle axe?
- How many kings have only one hand showing?
- How many kings are clean shaven?
- What do the queens hold in their hand?
- How many queens face to the left?
- How many queens don't have a dimple?
- How many jacks don't have a moustaches?
- How many jacks face to the right?
- How many jacks have two eyes?
- How many jacks have curly hair?
- What colour are the hats that the jacks wear?

5 Ask the participants how they went with the questions.

What to look out for

Insufficient motivation or explanation of the game—you can explain the game as being about learning, memory, communication, observation, your understanding of your environment and so on.

✏︎

✏︎

✏︎

Debrief

Key debrief ideas

1 You can see without noticing.

2 You may not know what you think you know.

Sample debrief questions

- How many times do you think you have seen a face card in your life?
- How would you define the difference between seeing and observing?
- What made this activity so difficult?
- How would the results change if we did the activity again?
- Were you surprised by how little you have noticed over the years?
- What other areas of your life might surprise you in a similar way?
- How often is there scope for new learning in something you've been doing for a long time? Why would that be important? How can training help??

✏︎

✏︎

✏︎

Walkies

15 minutes	Any number	Communication

Why it works for me

A kinaesthetic game that allows people to get out of the games room and to play the game in the actual workplace. When it's done well people can feel the difference and experience another way of doing things. It's magical when people are in exact sync and demonstrate their success.

Where it works best

Where there is some rapport established already—after lunch, or on the second or third days of a conference.

What you have to do

1   Make sure you have enough room for couples to walk around without bumping each other.

2   Get the participants to form pairs.

3   Ask Person A to walk, and Person B to follow behind and copy them as closely as possible. Tell the participants to consider:

- angle of the body to the ground and how stooped people are
- the length of the steps
- how the feet make contact with the ground
- the movement of the legs, arms and hips
- how they hold their head.

4   After a few minutes, ask Person B to tell Person A what they had to change to mimic them. For example, take smaller steps or lean forward more.

5   Get the partners to swap roles, repeat the exercise and feedback.

✐

✐

✐

What to look out for

- People who truly cannot see what to mimic, and who are completely out of touch with their bodies.
- Too much noise or running over time.

✐

✐

✐

Debrief

Key debrief ideas

1 Importance of seeing another's point of view.

2 Role of the body in communication.

Sample debrief questions

- How did you find this exercise?
- What made it easy or difficult?
- Did you have trouble keeping track of all the things the other person was doing?
- Do you notice what people are doing when they talk to you?
- What did you learn about how people use their bodies?
- Did it help show how others' experience of life is different from ours?
- What can you learn from walking in someone else's shoes? How can this help communication?
- After this exercise, what do you think the role of the body is in communication?
- What did you learn about yourself that you didn't know?

Stop Telling

30 minutes	10 minimum	Communication/leadership

Why it works for me

It allows participants to get out of their chairs, out of the room and even outdoors. It provides a clear opportunity for learning about hierarchy and its effect on communication. I've even seen a manager force someone to jump into a pool—which said a lot about the organisation.

Where it works best

In organisations with strong hierarchy and several levels in the training room, particularly when juniors can direct seniors. Works well in conferences.

What you have to do

1   Explain that the game explores communication and taking responsibility for what we say.

2   Get participants to:

- break into pairs
- nominate a Person A and a Person B.

3   Explain that:

- Person A stands behind Person B (about six inches)
- Person A tells Person B what to say, do and where to go
- Person B can't do anything without Person A telling them.

4   Ask the pairs to mingle and interact.

5   Tell participants to reverse roles and repeat the exercise.

✏

✏

✏

What to look out for

- Intervene if you hear silly orders being given.
- Monitor participant safety.
- Stop Person B chatting and not following instructions.
- Give clear instructions on the difference between Person A and Person B.

✏

✏

✏

Debrief

Key debrief idea

Highlight the problems of one-way communication and hierarchy and how taking responsibility can solve them.

Sample debrief questions

- Who enjoyed being Person A and why?
- Who enjoyed being Person B and why?
- What were the positive and negative points of being A or B?
- What does this say about the types of communication we use in the workplace?
- How can you apply this to what you've learnt in the training course today?

✏️

✏️

✏️

Variations

- Add observers.
- Give instructions in writing.

Where to Next?

10–15 minutes	Fewer than 8	Communication/teamwork

Why it works for me

This is an excellent rapport builder that demonstrates the importance of good communication and involves lots of movement and energy.

Where it works best

When people have worked together before or the group is a technical or problem-solving crowd.

What you have to do

1 Invite the participants to stand and form a tight circle in the centre of the room. Make the circle tight enough to almost reach across.

2 Ask them to raise their left hand in the air and point their right hand at the centre of the circle.

3 Ask them to lower their left hand and grab someone else's right hand, somewhere across the circle. Tell them that once they have made contact they can't let go.

4 Tell the participants to untangle themselves without breaking their grip. When untangled they should form another circle. It's OK that some people may face away from the centre.

✎

✎

✎

What to look out for

- Participants having played the game before.
- Anyone who is particularly shy or uncomfortable touching hands and arms.

✎

✎

✎

Debrief

Key debrief idea

Communication in problem solving and team roles.

Sample debrief questions

- Who initiated solving the problem? Why them?
- What could you have done to finish the exercise faster? How would this have made a difference?
- Did anyone feel they weren't listened to by the others? How did you feel about that?
- Were you all going in the same direction?
- How can you ensure you are all going in the same direction?
- What roles were there in the group?
- Did anyone take several roles?
- How do you take different problem-solving roles in the workplace?
- Can you see yourself playing any particular one at work?
- What might happen if you change the role you habitually take?

Variations

- Change the size of the groups involved.
- Have groups compete to untangle first.
- Have trial runs and allow for planning time, which can connect with planning and project management.
- Time each group.

The Visual Game

5 minutes	Any number	Communication/listening

Why it works for me

This is a short, fast game with a high fun factor, which gets people on their feet. Once, at a conference of more than 100 people, every single one did it incorrectly, which makes it a great motivator for listening.

Where it works best

When people are distracted or drained of energy, or need a change of learning style.

What you have to do

1 Invite everyone to stand.

2 Say, 'Listen carefully to what I say'.

3 Say, 'Make a circle with your thumb and second finger'.

4 Say, 'Now point your other three fingers in the air.

5 Say, 'Now place your hand and fingers under your chin' As you say this, put your hand on your cheek—most people will follow your visual lead, not the instructions.

What to look out for

• Make sure you notice how many do it correctly.
• Time it so that you move your hand to your cheek as you give the instruction.

Debrief

Key debrief idea

Distinguish listening as a special skill, and the power of visual communication.

Sample debrief questions

- How many of you put your hand on your cheek, not under your chin?
- Why do you think you did that?
- What role does the body have in our communication? How? (Quote communication as being 7% words, 38% voice and tone, 55% body language.)
- What consequences does this have for you in work?
- What do you need to learn in order to communicate better?
- How does this affect your all-important telephone communication?

✏️

✏️

✏️

Variations

- Use any symbol or body part (for example, instruct hand on elbow, and put it on your shoulder).
- Reverse it and get them to follow your visual lead (most will succeed).

What Can You Remember?

5 minutes	Any number	Communication

Why it works for me

This game works every time to demonstrate how mind and memory work and how they can affect communication. People love memory challenges so long as they're for fun; and this one provides strong evidence for chunking and organising information.

What you have to do

1 Prepare enough copies so half the group can have Sheet A and the other half Sheet B (see following pages—note that they have a different number of items).

2 Hand out equal numbers of Sheet A and B face down. If you can manage it, try to give senior people Sheet A.

3 Explain that the game is a bit of fun that helps show how we remember things.

4 Explain that the participants have 30 seconds to remember as many items on the sheet as possible.

5 Give the participants 30 seconds, and play some quiet thinking music that you stop as the time is up.

6 Tell them to turn the sheets over and give them a minute to write down what they can remember.

7 Ask the participants to exchange pieces of paper and score themselves.

8 Ask for the scores of people with a sheet marked A in the bottom corner. Then ask for the scores of those with the sheet marked B. Do it quickly.

9 Ask the participants to look at the other version of the list they have.

✐

✐

✐

What to look out for

• Protect people who may have very low scores.
• Don't dwell on the scores, get to debrief quickly.

✐

✐

✐

Debrief

Key debrief idea

Memory and communication are helped by organising and chunking information. Refer to the fact that short-term memory can only handle 5 $^+/_-$ 2 pieces of information (ie 3–7). When information is organised, people remember the detail. When it is random, people try to make a pattern and forget the detail.

Sample debrief questions

- What did you notice about the scores for people who had Sheet A as opposed to Sheet B?
- Why do you think the average was so different?
- How does organising information help us? What does it show us about memory? (Mention 5 $^+/_-$ 2.)
- How can this help you when you are writing notes? Thinking? Presenting information or talking to people?

What can you remember?

Memorise as many of these words as you can in 30 seconds.

shoe	pony
pink	Iran
snake	oak
Spain	affection
pine	lavender
like	handbag
swan	Afghanistan
Greece	life
gum	rooster
dislike	purple
black	palm
skirt	high heels
Egypt	pride
China	lipstick

A

What can you remember?

Without taking notes remember these words.

shoes	purple
gloves	pink
skirt	white
handbag	black
lipstick	grey
high heels	lavender
rooster	Spain
bull	Greece
cat	Afghanistan
swan	Egypt
mouse	Russia
lamb	China
gum	like
palm	dislike
willow	kindness
pine	life
maple	sex
jacaranda	pride

B

Fists

8 minutes	Any number	Communication

Why it works for me

A very simple game that highlights win-win negotiation and verbal and non-verbal communication. It works every time, providing a remarkable contrast in negotiation styles and outcomes—and those differences make people laugh.

What you have to do

1 Ask the participants to form pairs and stand up.

2 Ask person A in each pair to form two fists.

3 Explain that person B has to persuade person A to open their fists without touching them. Person B can say anything they like, but it's up to Person A when they open their fists.

4 Reverse the roles when everyone has opened their fists or reached an impasse.

✐

✐

✐

Debrief

Key debrief idea

Reveal elements of negotiation skills and the role of non-verbal communication in supporting the negotiation.

Sample debrief questions

• What sorts of argument did you use to persuade your partner to open their fists?
• Why did you choose those arguments? Which worked best?
• What, if anything, would you now do differently?
• What did you notice about the way the negotiators stood and what gestures they used? How did that make you feel?
• What did you learn from watching people try to persuade you?
• What does this show you about working with people?

✐

✐

✐

Variations

Allocate different postures and gestures to people for the attempted negotiation—explore the difference they make.

The Change Game

Why it works for me

It's a simple, concrete way of expressing what change is. It's also a good change of state because it gets people on their feet and laughing. You can link the game to any session involving any sort of change content.

Where it works best

With a physically oriented audience, especially when the energy level has dropped or it's the end of the day. It works well by relating to how one responds to doing things differently, as after a day's training.

What you have to do

1 Get the participants to:

   • stand up
   • find a partner.

2 Tell them to:

   • stay silent for one minute
   • look directly at their partner
   • observe the physical characteristics of their partner.

3 Ask them to:

   • turn their backs on each other
   • make five observable changes to their appearance
   • turn back and face their partner
   • try to guess the five changes.

4 Then ask them to turn their backs on each other again, and make 10 more changes (so that there are 15 changes in total).

5 Get them to face each other and try and guess the further changes.

6 Ask them if they are ready for more changes. (The answer should be No!)

7 Award a small prize to whoever was able to notice the most changes.

What to look out for

- Make sure the changes are demanding so they don't just enjoy the game, they also notice it is difficult.
- Keep the tempo fast, with changes closely following each other.
- You will aim to finish in less than four minutes, so you should be looking for an opportunity to close.
- Keep control of people who may want to take all their clothes off.
- Provide an opportunity to move to a different space to debrief and change back to how they were previously.

✏

✏

✏

Debrief

Key debrief idea

Relate the experience of change in the game to change in the workplace or their lives.

Sample debrief questions

- How did you feel about the number and pace of the changes?
- Do you ever feel that way anywhere else? (Look to connect to workplace.)
- Is there a limit to the amount of change you can handle?
- When you made the changes, did you tend to give something up or gain something? (Change doesn't have to be about losing.)
- Did you all remember the same number of changes? (People are at different levels of readiness for change.)
- Do our resources affect how we cope with forced change? (Not enough clothes can make the changes difficult.)
- Who immediately put themselves back to how they were at the start? What does that say about change?
- How can you apply this to what we've learnt in the training course today?

✏

✏

✏

Variations

- Change position and expression, rather than body and clothes only.
- Provide people with props and debrief on how they used (or didn't use) them.
- Get a participant to deliver the instructions.
- Make it so that people have to put things on, not take them off.

Power of Visualisation

10–15 minutes	Any number	Change

Why it works for me

It's a concrete example of what a clearly visualised goal can do, and it works equally well for all participants.

What you have to do

1 Invite the participants to stand.

2 Explain and demonstrate how to:

- stand with your feet squarely facing the audience
- swing your arm behind you at about waist height without moving your feet
- let your torso stretch as well
- take note of where you hand aligns to a spot on the wall.

3 Ask the participants to do the same, while giving a warning that it is a stretch and that they should be gentle with the motion.

4 Ask them to relax and visualise doing this exercise as hard as they can and going much further with their next stretch.

5 Ask them to do it again and notice the improvement in how far they can go.

6 Allow discussion among the participants about who got the greatest improvement.

What to look out for

- People pushing their bodies and causing injury—set up the idea of a gentle stretch that suits each individual.
- Sufficient space to do it easily.

Debrief

Key debrief idea

Visualising can improve performance because it allows you to practice perfectly, which you can't do in real life.

Sample debrief questions

- Did you find your stretch improved? Why do you think that was?
- What role do you think visualisation and relaxation played in getting a bigger stretch?
- How do you think visualisation helps performance? What about relaxation? What does this say about the barriers to better performance?
- Where can you use visualisation and relaxation to improve performance?
- Once we improve our performance, do we need to visualise any more?

✎

✎

✎

Variations

- Use more vigorous, sporting activities for younger audiences.
- Use small, plastic basketball sets and compare shot accuracy.

The Mentor

25 minutes	Any number	Leadership

Why it works for me

This exercise immediately keys into what is important for people—everyone has people who have influenced them in their lives. It's a concrete way of showing people how they can actually make a difference, and it does so by addressing emotions.

Where it works best

Where there is a mix of backgrounds and ages to reveal different mentoring elements.

What you have to do

1 Hand out copies of the Mentor worksheet (see page 81).

2 Ask the participants to:

- write the year of their birth and the current year at the ends of the timeline
- write on the timeline the names or initials of the people who have influenced them through their life
- mark their age or the time they were influenced or helped
- note down the important lessons they have learned from these people.

3 Ask any participants who are willing to share with the group the lessons they learned.

4 Get the participants to pool their ideas of what constitutes a good mentor.

5 Ask them to reflect on the extent they themselves have those qualities, and write down what they discover.

What to look out for

- Emotional reactions from remembering important, dead or dying mentors.

Debrief

Key debrief idea

Learning occurs all through life, not just at school. We can at any time be a positive influence on others around us.

Sample debrief questions

- Where did most of your important lessons take place? What does that say about school and learning?
- What sort of things make a good mentor? Why? Do they change as your age changes?
- What do you see in yourself that could make you a good mentor?
- How can you practically act as a mentor both inside and outside the workplace?
- Without saying them out loud, what values would you want to pass on to someone?
- How important are values in the workplace?

The Mentor worksheet

Dateofbirth _____ Datetoday

. . . .

My most important lessons were:

. . . .

. . . .

. . . .

. . . .

. . . .

. . . .

The Leadership Game

1 hour	Any number	Leadership

Why it works for me

It's an excellent game for reinforcing leadership theory because it allows participants to generate the content and reveals the gaps in what people are actually doing as leaders. It also reveals different views of leadership. By changing what is on each card, the game can work for any management issue.

What you have to do

1   Before the game prepare five cards for every participant (that is, 50 cards for a group of 10).

   • Each card has a statement about leadership on it.
   • Use at least seven statements.
   • Include statements people will accept, reject and feel ambiguous about. (For example: 'I want to use theory X in leadership', 'Leadership is about keeping people happy', 'Group decision making is a useful technique for developing standards'.)

2   Prepare a second batch of cards in the same way to act as an extra pile for people to draw from. Prepare as many for this batch as you did initially. Leave them face down on a table in the centre of the room.

3   Give each participant their five cards.

4   Ask the participants to sort their cards into those they agree with and those they disagree with.

5   Ask the participants to find a partner and trade the cards they disagree with for ones they agree with.

   • They must explain to their partner why they surrender or take a particular card.
   • Participants can exchange with as many people as they like.

6   After at least two trades, participants can exchange one of their cards for a fresh card from the pile in the centre of the room. They can only take the top card (without looking) and put their discard at the bottom of the pile.

7   Allow 30 minutes for the exchanges, or until the noise and action recedes.

8   Ask the participants to form groups of three or four and to agree on the five best cards. Get them to put their rejects in a pile for the group on the centre table.

✏️

✏️

✏️

What to look out for

- Too much intellectualising and debate.
- People who try to keep all the cards, rather than choosing only five.

Debrief

Key debrief idea

Discussion of cards chosen and the exchange process to show what people see as good leadership. Leading participants to productive views of leadership.

Sample debrief questions

- How did you find sorting the cards on your own?
- What did you use to guide you when you were sorting?
- What happened when you exchanged cards?
- Did everyone want the same things or was it easy to exchange?
- What did the groups decide leadership was?
- What does this say about leadership? What is it?
- How can leadership vary?
- What role does leadership have at work?
- How can you show leadership in the workplace?

Variations

- Have the participants prepare the cards—this will add to the time for the game, and you may have to edit the cards.
- Change the topic to something other than leadership—this game is versatile enough for any management theory.
- Use it again at the end of the session or course to show the changes in what participants see as leadership.

The Magnetic Chair

10 minutes	Even number	Goal setting

Why it works for me

A surprising and fun way to show the power of goal setting and focus. Participants are often amazed about the difference in what they do.

Where it works best

A big room and with a group that already has some rapport, perhaps late in the day or through a conference.

What you have to do

1 Divide the group into pairs with one chair between them or ask the participants to find a partner.

2 Tell them:

- Person A is to sit on the chair and try to stand up.
- Person B is to put their hands on Person A's shoulders and press down to stop them, or make it difficult for them to stand.
- Person B must ensure they do not hurt Person A.

3 After a few attempts, tell the participants to rotate roles and get them to try the same thing.

4 Return to Person A trying to stand, but ask them to focus on a goal just out of reach. For example, a door knob or curtain cord. They must give this goal their absolute attention.

5 Person B must apply the same amount of pressure as previously.

6 After this second try, ask both partners to discuss the difference from the first time.

7 Rotate roles and again allow for partners to discuss the difference.

✎

✎

✎

What to look out for

- People messing about and hurting each other, particularly young men.
- Not enough objects visible in the training room to allow for goals.

✎

✎

✎

Debrief

Key debrief idea

Things are more attainable when focusing on goals, not obstacles, and giving the goal strong focus.

Sample debrief questions

- What happened in each of the attempts? How was it different?
- Why do you think it was different?
- Where was your attention on each attempt?
- Does it make a difference to look at a goal rather than an obstacle? How? Is this true of anything else? What about at work?
- What does having a strong focus do for you? When is it useful?
- What role does focus have for solving problems?

➥

➥

➥

Variations

Particularly if you think the group may be rowdy, try asking them to lift an arm from a table, or a hand above horizontal.

Time Out

25 minutes	Any number	Goal setting

Why it works for me

This really succeeds when people suddenly realise how they are spending their time and that they don't want to do it that way. It gives a huge motivation to goal setting, prioritising and time management.

What you have to do

1 Before the session, prepare a flip chart with categories of how people spend their time. You could include:

- work
- friends and family
- interests and hobbies
- fun and relaxation
- exercise
- self-development
- socialising
- religious, spiritual or philosophical pursuit.

2 Give the participants a copy of the Time Out worksheet (see following page).

3 Tell them to carve up the pies to show how they use their time now and how they would like to. Display the flip chart to help them work it out.

4 Ask them to complete the sentences on the page.

5 Divide them into small groups to discuss what they might do to change how they allocate their time.

6 Bring the groups together and ask for insights into how we can manage our time.

✎

✎

✎

Debrief

Key debrief idea

Reveal how goal setting for a balanced life can make a difference.

Sample debrief questions

- Are you all doing what you want to do?
- Were you surprised by what you spend time on?
- What steps can you take to spend your time the way you want?
- How might the pie look for a high achiever? A happy person? A balanced person?
- How does having a balanced life affect your work?
- What happens if one aspect of life dominates?
- What is the key step to taking control of your time and doing what you want to do?
- How does it work?

Time Out worksheet

The way I spend my time:

I spend most time on:

. . . .

. . . .

. . . .

. . . .

The way I'd like to spend my time:

I would like to change:

. . . .

. . . .

. . . .

. . . .

I'll achieve this by:

. . . .

. . . .

. . . .

. . . .

Push Arms Down Game

15 minutes	Even number	Goal setting

Why it works for me

A simple game that involves everybody and provides great evidence of the role of mental and emotional state and focus on achievement. It has a broad debrief that you can relate to many different workplaces.

Warning: this exercise is isometric, which can be dangerous for people with heart conditions.

Where it works best

In male-dominated environments, as men tend to be more focused on being strong.

What you have to do

1   Warn the participants that this game involves some gentle exercise, and that people with heart conditions should be careful, or if they are concerned, act as observers.

2   Put the participants into pairs.

3   Explain that the game involves moving your arms and having your partner oppose the movement.

4   Demonstrate by taking a partner and:

- standing face-to-face with hands by your sides
- putting your hands on your partner's arms
- asking your partner to raise their arms into a cross position
- resisting the arm movement with a controlled force.

5   Ask Person A in the pairs to do the same thing. Give them 20 or 30 seconds.

6   When finished, ask Person A to:

- lift themselves into a positive mood
- change their stance so their weight is even and they are centred on the ground
- control their breathing and exhale on effort
- focus on their arms and see them moving beyond where they last reached
- commit to follow through and move their arm
- remember how they felt and what they saw when visualising.

7   Ask Person B to resist at the same level as the first time and repeat the exercise.

8   After this second attempt, ask both partners to discuss the difference.

9 Rotate roles, again allowing for partners to discuss the difference on the second attempt.

What to look out for

- Overly macho resistance.
- Fatigue.

Debrief

Key debrief idea

Our change of state and mental preparation can affect what we do.

Sample debrief questions

- What differences did you note about yourself?
- What differences did the resistors notice?
- If it didn't make a difference, why do you think that was?
- Where else is this sort of thing important and used often? (sports)
- Do you think it only applies to physical things?
- How can it help other activities? What about mental activities? At home or at work?

Apple and Straw Game

20 minutes	Any number	Goal setting

Why it works for me

This is the best game I've played by far. It's surprising, it's fun, it's a little bit messy and it gives real proof of how your attitude affects what you do. People are incredibly interested because they don't think it will work, and it gives you credibility when it does. When they see that demonstration, it's impossible to stop them from doing it. And when they actually do it, there is an Aha! learning that almost requires no debrief.

Where it works best

Everywhere.

What you have to do

1 Prepare by having an apple and a strong plastic straw (McDonald's style) for each participant.

2 Explain you're playing a game of putting the straw through the apple. You can build up people's disbelief if you like. Ask:

   - How many believe it's possible? Just difficult?
   - How often have you been faced with something you think is impossible?
   - It's possible with attitude and skill—what attitude? How would you acquire the skill?

3 Demonstrate putting the straw through the apple. You may want to demonstrate incompetence and fail a couple of times if you have a lot of people who lack confidence.

4 Tell the participants the key safety issues:

   - Hold the apple firmly on the sides between the thumb and index finger. Have no part of the hand underneath, and have the core of the apple horizontal.
   - Comfortably hold the straw vertically.
   - Swing firmly but not too hard.
   - Take a short swing only.
   - Go with the flow and follow through.

5 Ask the participants what it means for the future when they do this thing they think they can't do.

6 Ask the participants to put the straw through the apple.

✐

✐

✐

What to look out for

- Hand injuries—ensure people keep under the apple clear—repeat clear instructions and demonstrate how to hold the apple.
- People, particularly women, who don't believe they have the strength or co-ordination—tell a story of a small woman who surprised herself.

✏️

✏️

✏️

Debrief

Key debrief idea

Almost anything you want to choose:

- attitude + skill = good result
- importance of belief
- importance of follow through
- trying too hard can make something impossible
- self-limiting beliefs
- how changing state and consciousness to go with the flow allows us to achieve more
- our hidden powers.

Sample debrief questions

- How did you find the exercise?
- Could you do more than you expected?
- What did you learn from it?
- What happens when you have the right attitude?
- What happens when you try too hard?
- What does it feel like when it is just right?
- Did you really believe you could do it before you actually did?
- How do your beliefs limit what you do?
- How can you remove those limits?
- How does this allow you to view new challenges you meet?
- How can you meet those challenges?

✏️

✏️

✏️

Noughts and Crosses

15 minutes	Even number	Goal setting/creativity

Why it works for me

Immediately shows the benefit of having a strategy and of that strategy being a creative one.

Where it works best

Everywhere that goal setting and strategy are important. Use it at the beginning of the day around strategies for getting the most out of the day's learning.

What you have to do

1 Ensure you have prepared:

   • blank sheets of paper for every participant
   • coloured texts that they can use.

2 Divide the group into pairs.

3 Ask them to play on the paper as many games of noughts and crosses as they can in one minute.

   • Play some up-tempo music for the 60 seconds.
   • Allow no preparation of grids and so on.

4 At the end of 60 seconds, ask for the number of games played. Note the highest and lowest numbers.

5 Now ask the pairs to spend two minutes preparing a strategy for playing the most games of noughts and crosses in a minute. (Play some soft background music for the two minutes.)

6 At the end of the two minutes, say 'Now I expect you to improve by at least 10 games in the minute. Use your strategy to play as many games of noughts and crosses as you can.'

7 Start the minute and play some louder up-tempo music.

8 At the end of the minute ask for the number of games played and the improvement on the previous number.

What to look out for

- Odd number of people.
- Whingeing when people realise that they have unnecessarily limited themselves by completing games, playing them against each other and so on.

Debrief

Key debrief idea

Time to develop a strategy ensures better and more creative ways of reaching good results.

Sample debrief questions

- How did you benefit from having a strategy?
- For those of you who improved, what was your strategy?
- Would you have come up with that strategy by yourself? (For example, allowing incomplete games, writing small, playing against themselves.)
- Why would it be that people may do well in the first run and not in the second? (Successful strategy blinds to improvement.)
- If you are trying to reach some result, how is a strategy helpful?
- Where else do you need to reach results with what you are doing? (Work, home.)
- Aren't we better off with some strategy than none?
- The strategies we used depended on our idea of the instructions and rules of the game. When devising strategies how important are the rules you are used to being bound by?
- What is the best way to come up with new strategies?

Metaphors

40 minutes	Teams of 3	Goal setting

Why it works for me

This is a humorous game that combines all the energy and creativity of brainstorming with a neat way of revealing attitudes to what's going on in the business.

Where it works best

When all participants have a good command of English and everyone in the same group of three works together.

What you have to do

1 Divide the group into teams of three.

2 Explain that the game is in three parts:

   • a practice run where the participants talk about life
   • a real run where they talk about real and current work situations
   • another run where they talk about what they would like to have in their work situation.

3 Explain what a metaphor is: where one thing is compared with another, or said to be another, because they have some features in common.

4 Explain that in the practice section:

   • Person A says the first part of the metaphor 'Life is like ...'.
   • Person B completes the metaphor. For example, they may say '... a wave'.
   • Person C has to explain how life is like a wave. For example, 'Life's full of ups and downs, always changing, and dumps on you now and then'.

5 Ask the groups to complete the exercise themselves.

6 Rotate the roles so each person gets a chance to explain a metaphor.

7 Now have them talk about a current work situation rather than 'life'. For example, 'Project X is like ...', '... a circus', with 'too many things happening at once'.

8 Rotate roles so each person gets to explain a work metaphor.

9 Now have them talk about something they want in the workplace, rather than something they already have. For example, 'I want our department to be like ...'

10 Rotate the roles so each person gets to explain a future metaphor.

What to look out for

- People who don't understand metaphors and who don't understand the purpose of the game. Your introduction is vitally important.
- Super-concrete thinkers who have trouble understanding or creating metaphors.
- People from non-English-speaking backgrounds.
- Allow a lot of time for debrief.

✏

✏

✏

Debrief

Key debrief idea

In trying to come up with creative metaphors, people reveal their basic attitudes to the workplace.

Sample debrief questions

- How did you find having to come up with a metaphor?
- How did you find explaining someone else's metaphor?
- What metaphors did you come up with for your current work situations? How did they make sense? What did they reveal about your work? What were the key issues?
- How did creating a metaphor clarify what you want to change at work? Did it help you to think in new ways? What new paths can you see now? How many of them can you implement? How?

✏

✏

✏

Variations

Write down metaphors and draw them out of a hat for group discussion.

Let's Get Creative

20 minutes	12 minimum	Creativity/content reinforcer

Why it works for me

This is a great way to develop energy and creativity while having fun and reinforcing content already covered.

Where it works best

At the end of a day or the start of a following day, and in the evenings at conferences. It works well when the content is not very concrete—for example, about attitude change or diversity in the workplace.

What you have to do

1 Divide the participants into teams of three or four.

2 Tell the teams to create something like a story, song, rap, poem, play or dance that summarises the key points from the day's training.

3 Ask each team to make its presentation.

4 When each team is done, bring the group back together and thank them for their efforts.

✐

✐

✐

What to look out for

Groups that simply have no creative idea (give them a few tips).

✐

✐

✐

Debrief

Key debrief idea

Use the presentations as a starting point to talk about what has been learnt and where the group is going.

Sample debrief questions

- Congratulate the participants on their creativity.
- What do the presentations show you learnt today?
- What do you now know you need to look at in the future?
- When you let your creativity roam, what different angles does it present on the same information? How do those angles help us?

The Bizarre Animal Game

12 minutes	Teams of 4	Creativity

Why it works for me

The Anablp is such a bizarre animal that everyone loves finding out about it. But the game process is so open that there is a lot of scope for creativity and fun. The structure of the Anablp is also a great metaphor for anything that involves doing two things at once, especially monitoring process and content in presentations. When people don't believe me about the fish, I usually produce an article about it. You may want to photocopy something from an encyclopaedia. This really supports your credibility as a trainer—they tend to believe you after that.

What you have to do

1 Divide the group into teams of four.

2 Ask each team to come up with a creative definition of the Anablp.

3 Give the teams five minutes then ask them to present their definition to the group.

4 Ask the group to vote on what they think is the most convincing answer.

5 Explain what the Anablp is: a South African fish with four eyes—two above the water, looking for predators, and two below, looking for food.

Debrief

Key debrief ideas

1 The unlimited resource of our creativity.

2 Importance of monitoring process and content at the same time, focusing on both the big picture and the detail.

Sample debrief questions

• What did you notice about your team as you were coming up with an idea?
• Did you only have one idea? How easy was it?
• What does the difference in the definitions say about our creativity?
• When do we need to monitor two things at once?
• How can we monitor process and content at the same time?
• What skill does it take to keep many things in view?
• What happens if we only monitor process? (We don't get any information.)
• What happens when we focus too much on detail?
• How would keeping many things in view help you at work? In presentations?

✎

✎

✎

Variations

Use the Anablp as a metaphor for any multiskilled activity.

Build a Paper Plane

| 15 minutes | Any number | Creativity |

Why it works for me

It's an interactive, creative activity involving movement. This allows us to dismantle the roles participants are taking and get them into their bodies. There's scope for competition or groups if you want it. It also allows you to get across the importance of testing and piloting.

What you have to do

1 Tell the participants to:
   'Make a paper plane fly across the room and hit a target.'

2 Tell them the only restriction is that it has to be made of paper.

3 Get each participant or group to demonstrate their plane when they have finished.

4 If appropriate, award a small prize to those that hit the target or come closest.

✎

✎

✎

What to look out for

- Keep the participants moving fast.
- If in groups, encourage team brainstorming rather than leaving it to a single person.

✎

✎

✎

Debrief

Key debrief idea

You can think outside the square to get a better result.

Sample debrief questions

- Which plane did the best? Why?
- Can you think of a better design now you've seen all the others?
- What limited your creativity in designing? (Ideas of what a plane should be.)
- How did working with others affect your inventiveness?
- When is the most obvious way the best—and when isn't it?
- How does this relate to creativity in general? In the workplace?

Variations

- Change group sizes.
- Emphasise the competitive element.
- Add a time limit.
- Do it without speaking (since this makes it a good communication game as well).

Know the Answer

10 minutes	Any number	Creativity/communication

Why it works for me

This is a fun game that creates humour because most people get the same answer and because occasionally bizarre answers appear. Because it's a puzzle it intrigues, and it works well as a starter because its success gives you credibility to match the humour.

Where it works best

Large groups, conferences and other groups that have good rapport. This allows people to play the game without analysing it as they go along.

What you have to do

1 Stand in front of the group and explain that this is a quick game designed to show some features of communication.

2 Ask the participants to:

- pick a number between one and ten
- multiply it by nine
- add the two digits together
- subtract five
- match the correct letter of the alphabet to that number (A=1, Z=26)
- think of a country that starts with that letter
- think of an animal that starts with the second letter of that country
- think of the colour of that animal.

3 Check that everyone has a coloured animal from a country. If necessary, repeat the steps.

4 Ask how many people have a grey elephant from Denmark.

✏

✏

✏

What to look out for

- When people have a different animal/country, take the opportunity to say that communication is not perfect, but it is still directed by the questions you ask.
- People who forget their times tables.

✏

✏

✏

Debrief

Key debrief idea

When you communicate you can influence people to give the answer that you want without seeming to.

Sample debrief questions

- Why do you think that the exercise worked the way I wanted it to?
- What's the power of asking questions when you already know the answer?
- What's the role of questions in communicating and persuading people?
- What role can good questioning have in the work you do?

Name that Job

25 minutes	Any number	Creativity

Why it works for me

A good way to combine a few laughs and the joy of a puzzle with learning about the creative potential of groups.

What you have to do

1 Prepare a list of jobs on a flip chart or overhead (see page 107 for a list of example jobs).

2 Divide the group into teams.

3 Tell them you have an interesting dentist, because his name matches his job. His name is Phil MacCavity!

4 Ask them to create as many names as possible that match your list of jobs. The names:

   • should be plausible
   • can involve both first and surnames
   • can use initials and titles
   • can use puns and wordplay.

   For example: Astronomer   C. Farr
                   Criminal   Miss Creant
                   Accountant   Ben Counter

5 Ask the teams to share their lists with the whole group.

6 Score one point for each name, and extra points for creative names.

✐

✐

✐

What to look out for

   • Any team that is really stuck.
   • People who don't understand the game (give them the examples above).

✐

✐

✐

Debrief

Sample debrief questions

- Congratulate the participants on their creativity.
- How was the process of creating the names?
- Was it as difficult as you thought? Why?
- Did working in a group make it easier? Why?
- What worked well and what worked badly in the group?
- Do you think fun has a role in generating solutions? How?
- Can you use it at work? Do you have fun at work already?
- Do you access the creativity of the people at work?
- What do you think you miss out on by not using that creativity?

Variations

- Do it either with the group as a whole or with individuals working on paper.
- Job that Name is the flip side of this game.

Job that Name

5 minutes	Any number	Creativity

Why it works for me

This is a variation on Name that Job, but much easier. It's a fun, pun-filled, fast-moving game that forces participants to look at things differently.

What you have to do

1 Before you present the game, read the instructions to Name that Job.

2 Tell the participants about your dentist, Phil MacCavity, and that you want them to find jobs for all your other friends. The list on the following page provides a starting point for names, but you can make up your own. (Do NOT hand out this sheet.)

3 Ask the participants to come up with jobs to match the names in 60 seconds.

4 Stop them after 60 seconds and share the results.

✐

✐

✐

What to look out for

• People who don't understand (provide examples).
• People who get truly stuck.

✐

✐

✐

Debrief

Sample debrief questions

As for Name that Job.

Job that Name—trainer's suggested answer sheet

Do NOT hand out this sheet

Job Title	Name
Baker/Pastry cook	Min Spy
Painter/Make-up Artist	Matt Finish
Garbage worker	Chuck Binns
Lawyer	Sue McCase
Orchestra Conductor	Hans Waver
Motor Mechanic	Cam Shaft
Motor Mechanic	Carl Over
Soldier	Jack Boot
Road Worker	Doug Trench
Criminal	Rob Banks
Criminal	Con Man
Skier	Ben Zinees
Traveller	Sally Forth
Traveller	Aub Roamer
Traveller	Wanda Lust
Knitter	Pearl Cardigan
Banker	Penny Wise
Draftsperson	Drew Plan
Snake Charmer	Anna Conda
Dancer	Dizzy Head
Magician	Nathan Upmasleeve
Stunt person	Stan Din
Hippie	Ty Died
Paver	Tessie Late
Jockey	Winnie Post
Funeral Director	Mort Titian

The Opera House

1 hour	Groups of 5	Creativity

Why it works for me

A game that really allows people to get messy and be creative. In fact, it forces them into it. Because of that there is a huge level of energy and involvement, and as a finish it makes a session memorable. It's great watching people amaze themselves by what they can do.

Where it works best

At the end of conferences or highly emotional team-building sessions. Must have a lot of space and the freedom to make a bit of a mess.

What you have to do

1 Bring enough postcards of the Sydney Opera House so that each team can have one.

2 Prepare for each team:

- 2 jars of peanut butter
- 3 loaves of bread
- 1 bucket of water
- 1 bucket of instant mashed potatoes
- 1 pack of frankfurts
- 1 bottle of tomato sauce
- 3 plastic bowls
- 1 packet of toothpicks
- 1 packet of skewers
- 6 rice cakes
- 2 packets of Tim Tams
- 1 packet of Smarties
- Food colouring
- 10 Mini-Wheats
- Tablecloths, spoons, plastic sheet covers and aprons for each person.

3 Explain that for this game each group must build a replica Opera House out of the ingredients provided.

4 Give each group a postcard picture of the Opera House.

5 Tell them they have 25 minutes to get it done.

6 At the end of 25 minutes judge the best-looking Opera House, congratulate everyone on their efforts and get them to congratulate each other.

What to look out for

Mess!

✏️

✏️

✏️

Debrief

Sample debrief questions

- Who thought the task was impossible when you started?
- What did you learn as you actually put something together?
- Did you do something more creative than you thought you could?
- What can a group of motivated people create?
- What does this say about teams?

✏️

✏️

✏️

The Feast

1 hour	Groups of 8	Workplace difference

Why it works for me

The use of larger groups (8) generates both the rigidity and flexibility of the real world in the training room. Such big groups create cultural differences in the room, which works well. The key point of the game is being flexible in order to work effectively. Warning: this deals with a sensitive issue and can embarrass participants if it isn't run properly. Inexperienced trainers should consider a less risky game.

Where it works best

As part of a specific program on difference or culture. Where rapport has been well established. For example, at conferences in the evening.

What you have to do

1 Gather before the session:

- enough copies of roles 1 to 8, cut into strips so that each role is separate, for every group.
- box of tissues (to put beans on)
- two to three shallow dishes per group
- two packets of jelly beans per group
- individual towelettes.

2 Prepare the jelly beans and towelettes for each group.

3 Invite the participants to participate in a feast to celebrate the start/middle/end of the course.

4 Break the group into teams of eight.

5 Hand out to each participant their individual role that they must follow, and tell them not show it to the others. (See following page for roles.)

6 Allow them a few minutes to read and think about their roles, then invite them to 'party' according to their roles.

7 Invite the observer to add comments to the debrief after the game.

✏️

✏️

✏️

What to look out for

- People who don't follow their role.
- Any cases of aggression, embarrassment or confusion.
- People who want to eat and not play.
- Too much time spent on debrief.

✐

✐

✐

Debrief

Sample debrief questions

- How did you find the roles you played?
- How did the roles interact?
- Did you have any dilemmas in your role?
- Did individual 'cultures' affect the running of the group? How?
- How did you feel about the other roles?
- What did rigidly following the roles do to the group?
- How did people react?
- Was anyone offended or frustrated? Why?
- For groups where it worked, what did you do?
- What could you do to make it work?
- How can you apply this when you deal with people who are different from you?

✐

✐

✐

Variations

- Treat it as a one-day course.
- Change the number or description of roles.

The Feast role descriptions

Role 1

In your culture it's forbidden to take food from a plate from which someone else has already taken food. Your culture doesn't allow you to point this out to the group, nor would you ask anyone to give you some of their food after the bowl is emptied. In your culture, it's offensive to discuss people's age in public. Anyone who asks about age in the group is committing a serious breach of your customs.

Role 2

In your culture, nothing coloured blue, orange or purple may be eaten. However, you prize food that is white, red or black. These colours are so valued that they're worth twice as much as any other colours, and trading for red, white or black food is widely practised. In your culture, it's essential that everyone be served and eat at the same table. It's offensive for anyone to eat apart from the whole group and on this issue you insist on everyone observing your customs.

Role 3

In your culture, the oldest person in the group would share out the food equally. As the oldest person present, you expect everyone to respect this custom. If that doesn't happen, it's a serious breach of your customs, which is punishable by offenders forfeiting any food they take without waiting for you to carry out the ritual. You also expect that people respect your age by giving you any black or green food.

Role 4

In your culture, sharing food from a common bowl is acceptable, but only after everyone has washed their hands. You're in a mixed cultural group and must explain the custom and insist that it be carried out before the meal begins. You're happy with any colours, as long as everyone has an equal quantity.

Role 5

In your culture, it's forbidden to eat or talk with the opposite sex during a meal. Indeed, it's offensive to you to sit at a table in a mixed group. You insist that the food be divided in half, and placed in two bowls—one for men, and one for women. Each group should then divide the food equally among its members.

Role 6

In your culture, the food is divided by starting with the youngest person who takes one piece, the next oldest takes two pieces and so on, with everyone in rising order of age taking one more piece than the person before them. The colour of the food is irrelevant.

Role 7

In your culture, it's perfectly acceptable to grab as much as you can, disregarding the needs of others. However, having piled up your food, you can't start eating until all the food has been taken. It's quite acceptable to trade from your pile with anyone who wishes to get special colours in their food. You should initiate this role play by talking as much as you want. Don't wait for anyone to clarify the rules or explain their role.

Role 8—Observer

Please watch the exercise and comment on:

- listening and taking into account other participants' needs
- any non-participants and how the group handled this
- discomfort, frustration or embarrassment
- ways in which the group could have co-operated more effectively.

Lost at Sea

20 minutes	Any number	Workplace difference

Why it works for me

This game allows people to share personal values in a 'non-mushy' way and opens up a discussion of difference that isn't personally directed.

Where it works best

Wherever there is some degree of conflict or personality clash, either in the training room or the workplace. It also helps if there is a variety of personality types in the training room.

What you have to do

1 Ensure you have paper and a pen for every participant.

2 Ask the participants to imagine they have been marooned on a desert island.

3 Give each participant their piece of paper and pen.

4 Ask them to choose six people they want to be marooned with. They can be alive or dead, famous or not. Allow five minutes for people write down the names.

5 Invite each person in turn to list their choices and explain their reasons for choosing those people.

What to look out for

- Ditherers and slow workers.
- Dismissive or contemptuous remarks about people's choices—ensure you set up a supportive audience for comments before the game starts.

Debrief

Key debrief idea

Attractive and unattractive qualities in others and how to deal with both.

Sample debrief questions

- What qualities seem to be common to the people we've chosen?
- Why are those qualities attractive?
- What do our choices say about us?
- What does this mean we don't like in people?
- Is it important to like the people you work with? Why?
- If we're stuck with people we don't like, how can we work better with them?

Variations

- Pick six people you don't want to be on the island.
- Pick six people from work to be on the island. (Take care, this could be dangerous!)

Most Frequented Fast-Food Outlets in the USA

1 hour	Teams of 5–7	Teamwork

Why it works for me

Simple way of revealing team behaviours and has a self-directed debrief. Versatile enough to use with any list.

Where it works best

With people who work together and before you present teamwork content, so participants don't disguise their team behaviours.

What you have to do

1 Prepare enough ranking sheets for everyone in the group (see following page).

2 Form groups of 5–7.

3 Give everyone a ranking sheet and ask them to rank the fast-food outlets in order of the most frequented outlets in the USA.

- The most frequented is ranked 1, the least 10.
- Ask them to write the rankings in column 1 of their ranking sheet.
- Allow 15 minutes to complete this task.

4 Ask them to come together and rank the fast-food outlets as a team.

- Ask them to write this in column 2 of the ranking sheet.
- Allow 35 minutes for this task.

5 Focus the group on you and read out the expert's ranking.

- Get the participants to write down the expert ranking in column 3 and then calculate columns 4 and 5.

6 Flip chart the difference between the individual score and the team score for each participant. Group the information by teams.

✎

✎

✎

What to look out for

- Participants who dominate and participants who are too shy to participate fully.
- Confusion over the calculation of the difference.

✏️

✏️

✏️

Debrief

Key debrief idea

Learning from the process of getting a team result from individual results.

Sample debrief questions

- How did you find trying to come to a team consensus?
- Did anyone feel that they didn't say what they wanted to? Why? How did you feel about that?
- What did you notice about the team discussion?
- What helped the team to reach consensus?
- What hindered the team?
- What can individuals do to increase the team's effectiveness with consensus decisions?

✏️

✏️

✏️

Variations

- Have fewer ranking items.
- Change the list so it can involve anything, for example, the 10 most dangerous jobs.

Most Frequented Fast-Food Outlets in the USA—ranking sheet

	1 Your Individual Ranking	2 The Team's Ranking	3 Expert's Ranking	4 Difference Between 1&3	5 Difference Between 2&3
1 Hooters					
2 Pizza Hut					
3 Wendy's					
4 Donut King					
5 McDonald's					
6 Subway					
7 Burger King					
8 Taco Bell					
9 Hot dog stands					
10 KFC					
Total Scores					

Your score   Team score

Most Frequented Fast-Food Outlets in the USA—correct answers

1 McDonald's
2 Burger King
3 Pizza Hut
4 Hot dog stands
5 KFC
6 Hooters
7 Donut King
8 Taco Bell
9 Wendy's
10 Subway

The Blind Walking Race

50 minutes	12 or more	Teamwork/body

Why it works for me

This game is a combination of trust and communication. It's magic when people believe in their partner so much they walk at normal pace, and the experience can strongly bond teams. It also opens people up to extending and using their senses and higher levels of concentration.

Where it works best

When you have lots of space and need to generate some energy and trust to move on to the next content area.

What you have to do

1   Bring a supply of blindfolds and broom handles.

2   Break the group into pairs.

3   Blindfold one participant in each pair.

4   Give the blindfolded participant a long stick or broom handle.

5   Place obstacles such as chairs and boxes around the room.

6   Ask the partner to guide the blindfolded participants around the room.

7   Get the partners to switch roles and do the exercise again.

✏️

✏️

✏️

What to look out for

• Participant safety and irresponsible participants.
• Ways of varying the game as you play it to make it more interesting or to create new versions.

✏️

✏️

✏️

Debrief

Sample debrief questions

- How did your other senses help when you lost your sight?
- What did you visualise?
- Was it like seeing?
- How hard was it to trust your partner? What was it like once you did?
- Did you find you had to concentrate?
- What was different about the concentration? (active listening and feeling)
- Where do you have to rely on others in a trusting way? (work and home)
- Is this trust important?
- What do you have to do to establish trust in your daily life?

✏

✏

✏

Variations

- Once people have established trust, possibly put people into a race.

The Bum Race

10 minutes	Any number	Teamwork

Why it works for me

Only applies when you have a clear brief from the client to provide fun. This works in the evening at conferences where participation is optional. It's a fun game that gets the body involved and teamwork happening.

Where it works best

With younger groups or teens that know each other well. Conference groups with great rapport, energy, humour and a little alcohol often love it.

What you have to do

1 Ensure the participants are wearing comfortable, casual clothes.

2 Invite the participants to form into groups of four.

3 Ask them to sit on the floor in a relay formation (two at each end of the course).

4 Explain that they have to bounce across the floor in a relay race.

5 Start the race with a clap, whistle or yell. Participants then race across the floor to the other end of the course by bouncing on their behinds, or 'walking' on their buttock cheeks.

✏️

✏️

✏️

What to look out for

- Insufficient rapport to get people involved.
- People dressed inappropriately (skirts).
- Complaints over lack of connection to anything—be sure to frame it as fun and fun only; proceed only if you have client support.
- Participants becoming too rowdy.

✏️

✏️

✏️

Debrief

Key debrief idea

Difficult as this is a fun-only game. Choose from any of the debrief directions below.

Sample debrief questions

- Who felt uncomfortable participating? Why?
- What allowances do we have to make for people with different resources (eg clothes)?
- Why didn't anyone offer a solution to this problem?
- What is the role of fun in team building? In learning?

Feelings and Emotions

30 minutes	2 teams of 5	Teamwork

Why it works for me

This game offers positive experiences of expressing something participants don't often access. It gives a great debrief about people not expressing what they feel.

Where it works best

Presentation skill courses that focus on conflict and emotional awareness and control.

What you have to do

1 Prepare a stack of cards with an emotion written on each card (eg love, hate and so on).

2 Divide the group into two teams of around five.

3 Put the stack of cards on a table or box between the two groups.

4 Ask a participant from Group A to take the top card and act out the emotion for the other group.

   • Keep this to a time limit, say one or two minutes.
   • If Group B correctly guesses the emotion, they receive 10 points.

5 Now ask a participant from Group B to act out an emotion for Group A.

6 Rotate the acting opportunities between the members of the two groups.

7 Stop after 20 minutes and announce the winning team.

✐

✐

✐

What to look out for

• People who pick a card that's too difficult (jump in and offer another card).
• People who get stuck.
• Actors who deliberately make it difficult to guess.

✐

✐

✐

Debrief

Key debrief idea

Awareness of the feelings of others and non-verbal communication.

Sample debrief questions

- How do we learn how others feel?
- What are the key ways people communicate feelings?
- How important are body language and non-verbal communication?
- How do you think they work?
- What use can you make of people's non-verbal signals? (Relate to work.)
- How much of our communication at work is non-verbal?
- How can this help us to work better with the emotions of our colleagues?

Variations

- Provide a small prize for the winning team.
- Use charades to help verbalise anything or any issue.
- Get participants to choose their own emotion about the workplace.

The Seven Ps

10 minutes	10 minimum	Teamwork/difference

Why it works for me

It's one of those games with a magic, fun moment. When people guess who a card represents there's a lot of laughter and a realisation that we know people better than we think. The game can also be turned to relate to other topics with different Ps. It builds relationships and because it runs over the day, it keeps an ongoing interest in the sessions.

Where it works best

Large groups that know each other. Especially good for mid-sized to large corporations.

What you have to do

1 Hand out a card to each participant.

2 Write the seven Ps on a flip chart/overhead:

   • person you would like to meet
   • politician you dislike the most
   • paperback you would most like to read
   • pet you wanted as a kid
   • pet peeve
   • place you would most like to be today
   • phobia.

3 Ask the participants to write their seven Ps on their card.

4 Collect the cards and shuffle them.

5 Select one and read it out.

6 Ask the participants to guess the author and write it down on a piece of paper.

7 Put the card you read at the back of the pile.

8 During the course of the day read out all the cards. Keep them in the order you read them for a 'Big Reveal' at the end of the day.

9 Reread the cards at the end of the day in the same order, asking after each 'Who guessed that this was XXX?'

✏
✏
✏

What to look out for

- Inappropriate answers—read silently to check before you read them out.
- Judgmental responses as you read out a card—keep judgement out of the game.
- People deliberately choosing the opposite of their preference.

✎

✎

✎

Debrief

Key debrief idea

Reveals diversity in teams, unknown depth in people, and how well we know each other.

Sample debrief questions

- Who was surprised by some of the cards? Why?
- Was it easy to pick out some people?
- Did you pick more or fewer than you thought you would?
- What does the range of answers suggest?
- Do you think this difference is useful? (Mention the power of diversity to generate solutions.)
- Do you feel you know the people in the group better?
- How is that useful?

✎

✎

✎

Variations

- Offer a prize for the person with the most correct guesses.
- Include a phantom card.
- Include one for yourself.
- Change the Ps to relate to any particular area (for example, management styles).

Pass the Deck

10–15 minutes	Any number	Teamwork/leadership

Why it works for me

A good game to show the tension between time and quality. There's a lot of movement even though people remain sitting. It's also a game with no advantage to gender, strength or co-ordination, and little set-up required.

What you have to do

1　Ask the participants to form groups of five to seven.

2　Tell them to put their chairs side-by-side in a line, so that each group can see the other groups.

3　Put a full deck of cards at one end of each group.

4　Explain that the object of the game is to pass all cards from one end of the line to the other.

- The first player must pick up a single card and pass it to the closest hand of the next player.
- That player must pass it to the closest hand of the next player and so on.
- The final player must put each card in a neat pile at the end of the line.

5　Explain that:

- if a player drops a card, the team must wait until the player picks it up
- no-one can hold more than one card at once
- all cards must be passed.

6　Allow the teams five minutes to plan their strategy.

7　The team that finishes first is the winner.

✏

✏

✏

What to look out for

- Establish quality standards at the start.
- Ensure people in groups are involved at the preparation stage.
- Emphasise the competitive aspect to create time pressure.

✏

✏

✏

Debrief

Key debrief idea

How quality is affected when we respond to time pressures and the role of planning.

Sample debrief questions

- How did the winning team win?
- Was the planning time useful? How did you use it?
- What would you now plan to do differently?
- Did anyone drop cards? If they did, why did they?
- Did you put yourselves under pressure? How did that affect you?
- How much of your work is done under pressure?
- How can you perform better under pressure?

✏️

✏️

✏️

Variations

- Pass any item.
- Change the standards or make the process more complicated.

Stand or Fall

20 minutes	10 minimum	Teamwork/communication

Why it works for me

It's a simple game that gets participants involved and forces them to take a stand. It cuts to the core quickly to reveal the issues you choose to address.

Where it works best

You get the most from it under time pressure and where people are isolated individuals that cohere into a team.

What you have to do

1 Prepare a series of questions that have to be answered True or False.

- Make the questions range from easy to difficult.
- The questions can be on general knowledge or deal with a training topic.

2 Divide the participants into two teams.

3 Explain that when you read the questions the teams must:

- discuss and agree on an answer
- all answer in unison by raising their hands (for true) or crossing their arms (for false).

4 Read the questions one-by-one.

5 The first team to respond to each question correctly gets a point.

6 The team with the most points is the winner.

✐

✐

✐

Debrief

Key debrief idea

Benefits of teamwork and the problems of self-censorship in group discussion.

Sample debrief questions

- What was the benefit of working in the team?
- How often could the team answer a question you couldn't?
- Did anyone censor their views when they were playing? Why?
- Who accepted the team answer when they disagreed?
- How did that make you feel about the team?
- What strengths do teams bring to the workplace?
- Do any of you currently use these strengths at work? How?
- What barriers are there to teamwork?
- What can you do to make the most of the power of teams?

✎

✎

✎

Variations

- Increase the number of teams.
- Change topics for the questions to relate to training subjects.

Feedback and Teams

30 minutes	10 minimum	Teamwork/communication

Why it works for me

It reveals what is often not said in team building (both positive and negative) and succeeds through its honesty. A great way to finish off conferences and team building sessions, and to anchor what has happened in the previous days or sessions. It's magic when people access their emotions. In one course I ran the participants refused to leave the room and many kept the paper and framed it. Warning: this game deals with a sensitive issue and can embarrass participants if it isn't run properly. Inexperienced trainers should consider a less risky game.

Where it works best

At the end of a seminar or conference, where participants have some established relationships. It is particularly useful in sessions made up of people who work together.

What you have to do

1 Arrange the participants' chairs in two lines directly opposite each other.

2 Write on a piece of flip chart paper:

   • 'The thing I like most about you'
   • 'The thing I need more of from you'
   • 'The gift I would most like to give you'.

3 Ask participants to move around the chairs speaking for one minute to each person, telling them the answers to the three questions.

4 When the noise dies down and people feel they have spoken to everyone, bring the group together and discuss the comments people received.

5 Give participants an opportunity to write down the feedback they received.

What to look out for

- People who are overly negative (take them aside and re-frame the exercise for them, making it more positive).
- Any angry responses (intervene immediately).
- People forgetting the three things (put the flip chart where it can be seen).
- Keep people moving from person to person.

✏️

✏️

✏️

Debrief

Key debrief idea

Identifying people's strengths and weaknesses, and their experience of being told what their strengths and weaknesses are.

Sample debrief questions

- How did you find telling people these things and being told them? Why?
- What strengths do you now know you have that you didn't know before?
- What weaknesses could you improve on?
- What benefits do you get from honest feedback?
- How would this be important at work?
- Where does it make a difference now?
- What would change if there was more honest feedback at work?

✏️

✏️

✏️

Variations

Put a piece of paper on the back wall for each participant and let people write comments on each.

Resourceful State Game

10 minutes	12 minimum	Teamwork/creativity

Why it works for me

It's a fast way for people to get to know one another that reveals how much they can do with very little. It often creates a lot of movement and energy as people empty their handbags and pockets.

Where it works best

When people don't know each other very well, and people have their bags in the training room.

What you have to do

1   Divide the participants into teams of four.

2   Ask them to find objects in the room that begin with each letter of the alphabet. For example:

- A is for apple
- B is for bag
- C is for car keys.

3   First team to finish wins. Ask the winning team to read their list to the rest of the group.

What to look out for

- Putting all the resourceful people in the same group.
- Problems getting XYZ objects.
- Spelling mistakes.

Debrief

Key debrief idea

Learning about people through their possessions and how creative we can be when under pressure.

Sample debrief questions

- How difficult was it to come up with something?
- What was the best way to work to an answer?
- Did you think you would be able to do it? Why?
- What did this show you about being resourceful in a team?
- What did you learn about your team members?
- How could the resourcefulness of a team make a difference at work?

✏

✏

✏

Variations

- Change the speed or time available.
- Use fewer letters (for example, A–M only).
- Ask for more items for each letter.
- Award double points for XYZ.

Mish-Maths

40 minutes	Teams of 5–6	Communication/leadership

Why it works for me

A great model of a complex task where everyone can contribute something. People can only succeed working as a team, and those that succeed fastest do so because of good leadership. Gets the teamwork point across every time.

Where it works best

Literate workplaces where people aren't scared of numbers or anything that looks like algebra (even if it isn't).

What you have to do

1 You will need the following items to play the game:

- a desk, table or flip chart for each team to calculate and draw on
- some A4 rough paper
- envelopes containing team member instructions for five members of each team (see pages 136–7)
- material for creating a large picture in several colours—flip chart paper and felt-tipped markers in red, black, blue, green and yellow
- answers (which you, as trainer and quality controller, hold).

2 Explain to everyone that the object of the game is to help the person nominated as Team Leader to draw a single diagram following certain rules. The first team whose Team Leader completes the diagram, wins.

Team Leaders will not be able to make their diagrams until they have the information that only their entire team can provide. They will need to combine the team's input to produce a single composite diagram.

3 Identify each team member clearly as Team Leader, Team Member A, B, C, D and E. The Team Leader may also act as a Team Member. Distribute the code envelopes to each Team Member. (See pages 136–7.) Give Team Leaders a few sheets of A4 paper to sketch on. They may need to do a couple of preliminary sketches first, to help them build the diagram progressively.

4 Ask them to start when they're ready. You take no further action. When a team announces that they've finished the task, check that the rules have been met. If not, ask the players to finish it, but don't tell them yet what the omissions are. Let them try to work it out for themselves.

✏️

✏️

✏️

What to look out for

Teams that get completely lost or whose leader cannot lead (good for debrief, but bad for a long exercise).

✎

✎

✎

Debrief

Key debrief idea

1   Joint problem solving creates mutual benefits because each member of a team can contribute something: knowledge, effective communication, good relationships, enthusiasm and so on.

2   Different leadership styles of team leaders.

Sample debrief questions

- What did you find out about working as a team?
- When everyone has something to contribute do you have to work as a team?
- What benefits do you get from joint problem solving? How does this apply to the workplace?
- Does one person ever have all the information relevant to a problem?
- What sort of leadership styles did the team leaders have? How did they work?
- What team environment did the different styles create?

✎

✎

✎

And the answer is:

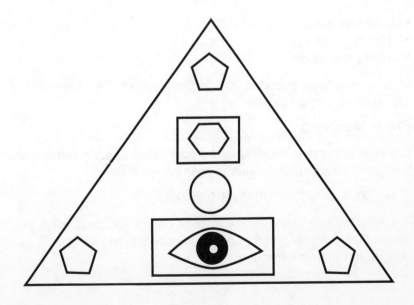

Mish-Maths team member roles

Instructions for Team Member A

You have important information for your Team Leader, without which the group task can't be completed. This is your information:

17 – H(2)Xs = 9A + Bs = 11(2)Xs.

You have to understand what it means before you pass it on. For this, you'll need other team members' special knowledge, just as they'll need yours to understand their information.

Your special knowledge is:

- M means one
- H means two
- S means three
- 17 means four.

As soon as you've decoded your information with the help of your colleagues, take it to your Team Leader.

Instructions for Team Member B

You have important information for your Team Leader, without which the group task can't be completed. This is your information:

4M(5)(10)22H(2)Xs + 18Bs = 11(5)(10)

You have to understand what it means before you pass it on. For this, you'll need other team members' special knowledge, just as they'll need yours to understand their information.

Your special knowledge is:

- (2) means red
- (5) means blue
- C means black
- 19 means green
- 18 means yellow.

As soon as you've decoded your information with the help of your colleagues, take it to your Team Leader.

Instructions for Team Member C

You have important information for your Team Leader, without which the group task can't be completed. This is your information:

H(2)Xs = 12MC23 + 4MC13 12M(2)X

You have to understand what it means before you pass it on. For this, you'll need other team members' special knowledge, just as they'll need yours to understand their information.

Your special knowledge is:

- B means pentagon (Bs is plural)
- 13 means hexagon
- P means cross
- 23 means triangle
- (10) means circle
- X means oblong (Xs is plural)
- E means eye.

As soon as you've decoded your information with the help of your colleagues, take it to your Team Leader.

Instructions for Team Member D

You have important information for your Team Leader, without which the group task can't be completed. This is your information:

4M19E 12MX + 18Bs > (5)(10)

You have to understand what it means before you pass it on. For this, you'll need other team members' special knowledge, just as they'll need yours to understand their information.

Your special knowledge is:

- 12 means inside
- 11 means outside
- 22 means between
- > means is/are larger than
- 9 means on top of
- 4 means there is, or there are
- A means each other.

As soon as you've decoded your information with the help of your colleagues, take it to your Team Leader.

Instructions for Team Member E

You have important information for your Team Leader, without which the group task can't be completed. This is your information:

S18Bs = 12C23 + 4M(2)P 12M 18B

You have to understand what it means before you pass it on. For this, you'll need other team members' special knowledge, just as they'll need yours to understand their information.

Your special knowledge is:

- – means subtract
- + means and
- = means are.

As soon as you've decoded your information with the help of your colleagues, take it to your Team Leader.

The Balloon Game

15 minutes	Even number	Teamwork/communication

Why it works for me

This generates a ridiculous amount of laughter, breaks barriers and helps build a team. It reinforces rapport and is a good way of celebrating what groups have achieved.

What you have to do

1 Ensure you have enough balloons so each person in the room can have one. Have equal numbers of the four colours: red, white, blue and green.

2 Ask the participants to blow up their balloon.

3 Explain that they have to:
- find a place around the room
- keep the balloon up off the ground using only their feet
- try to knock other people's balloons down with their feet while keeping theirs up
- continue until only one person is left.

4 Get the colour groups to strategise about how one of their colour can be the last person.

5 If anyone's balloon hits the ground, they have to pick it up and go to the back of the room.

6 Set a time limit of two minutes to ensure people try to knock down other's balloons.

7 When one person is left, tell the participants they must find a partner and burst their balloon with their partner. It must be a team effort. Rule out stomping, pins, squeezing etc. (People usually burst it in a hug.) Get people to check with you if they aren't sure.

8 Debrief when all balloons are burst.

✏

✏

✏

What to look out for

- People using their hands and heads to keep their balloon up.
- Overly enthusiastic players.

✏

✏

✏

Debrief

Key debrief ideas

1 How people felt about ruining the others' efforts.

2 How creatively they resolved bursting the balloon as a team.

3 Connect to anything related to teams and competition.

Sample debrief questions

- How did you feel about forcing others out of the game? Was it difficult?
- How did it feel when someone pushed your balloon to the floor?
- What sort of effect can anger have in teams?
- How did you deal with bursting the balloon as a team?
- Was it difficult to come up with a method?
- Did working as a pair help?
- What happens when the only way to do something is together?

Variations

- Get participants to help balloons of their colour to stay up.

Hands Off!

30–40 minutes	Any number	Teamwork

Why it works for me

This is a good way of introducing some of the basic ideas of sexual harassment. It provides a good foundation for training on company policy.

Where it works best

When people know each other already, and are at the same or similar level in the corporate hierarchy.

Special Note: This issue could not be more serious. It is your responsibility to ensure that participants treat the issues discussed here (and their fellow participants) respectfully. I would recommend that you make yourself thoroughly familiar with the group through extensive pre-course analysis to uncover any issues that may affect the productive running of the game (eg a participant with a sexual harassment or discrimination claim currently being heard). I would also recommend that you familiarise yourself with the Equal Opportunities Commission's (EOC's) Code of Practice. If you are comfortable with your knowledge of the group, your ability to deal with the issues raised and your knowledge of the recommended Code of Practice then, with careful preparation, give the game a go. It's a great one! While the subject is serious, this does not mean that the game should be carried out in a sombre and black mood. Much better results will be achieved for all if a good-humoured, warm and mutually supportive air is generated.

What you have to do

1   Prepare several sets of cards with harassment types written on them (see the following page for some examples).

2   Divide the group into teams of four or five.

3   Give each team a set of cards.

4   Ask them to sort the cards in ascending order, from least to most objectionable behaviour.

5   Ask the teams to report their ranking to the group.

6   Encourage discussion about different rankings and why one situation may be worse than another.

7   Put the group back into teams and ask them to come up with appropriate responses to each situation:

   • as the person in the situation or
   • as the supervisor of the person in the situation.

8   Get the teams to report their responses to the group.

9   Discuss which is the best response and highlight assertive responses and body language.

What to look out for

- Personal experience of harassment dominating the session.
- Team presentations taking too long.
- Joking responses to harassment.
- Participants being embarrassed by discussing situations that upset them or have occurred to them in the past.
- Side conversations occurring during the game about other individuals within the group. Ask those involved to focus on game participation.

✏

✏

✏

Debrief

Sample debrief questions

- Were any of you surprised by what might be harassment?
- How much disagreement was there about what constitutes harassment? Why?
- How differently did you rank the situations? What does that mean?
- What sort of responses are appropriate?
- Has your view of harassment changed? (no answer required)
- How can you apply this awareness to how you work?

✏

✏

✏

Sexual harassment situations

- The men in your office make remarks about your breasts.
- A stranger breathes heavily down the telephone.
- Your boss stares at your legs.
- A group of people whistle when you walk past.
- Your sports coach keeps putting an arm around you, telling you that you're cute.
- Someone at work keeps telling dirty jokes and makes suggestive remarks.
- Staff are allowed to have nude or sparsely clad pin-ups around the walls and workstations.
- Your trainer keeps brushing up against you and telling you how nice you look.
- A co-worker grabs your buttocks when you walk past.
- Women comment on 'how you fill your shorts'.
- At office parties, someone keeps squeezing your hand when you pass them some food or drink.
- Your boss tells you that if you're 'very nice', you'll get a promotion/raise.
- Someone in the elevator runs a hand up your leg.

Animal Noises

20 minutes	20 minimum	Teamwork

Why it works for me

A fun way to approach what makes teams important and the different feelings people have about being in teams. It asks people to be a little silly, but gives them the comfort of doing it blindfolded—which makes it something people enjoy and remember.

What you have to do

1   Prepare blindfolds for each participant in advance.

2   Clear the furniture from a large space.

3   Blindfold each participant.

4   Give each participant an animal role that has a distinctive call or sound. For example, assign five people for each of:

   • cat
   • dog
   • pig
   • cow
   • chicken.

5   Ask the participants to make the noise their animal makes and then to group themselves with the other animals that have the same call. They can make no other noises.

6   After 10 or 15 minutes call a halt and ask people to take off their blindfolds.

   ✏

   ✏

   ✏

What to look out for

   • Players who refuse to engage in the game.
   • Players who get frustrated and give up.

   ✏

   ✏

   ✏

Debrief

Sample debrief questions

- Did anyone feel silly playing the game?
- How did you feel about playing the game?
- How did you find your fellow team members?
- How did you feel when you found your group?
- How important was it to you to find your team?
- If people have different levels of needing to belong, how does that affect teams?
- What about loners in teams?
- What role did listening play in the game?
- How important is listening and communication in putting a team together? In keeping a team together?

✏️

✏️

✏️

Variations

Have one person be a duck when there are no other ducks—debrief on the experience of being left out of the group.

Our Strengths

25 minutes	Even number	Teamwork/opener

Why it works for me

This game combines many features which allow you to use it as an opener, a team builder or a confidence booster. It's a simple way to show how strengths relate to success, and to suggest that other successes can follow from those strengths. It's a great finisher for the day to send people home with positive thoughts about themselves and about the training session.

What you have to do

1 Prepare in advance a roots and fruits handout for each participant (see page 146).

2 Distribute a handout to each participant.

3 Ask the participants to reflect on themselves and their strengths and successes.

4 Ask them to write a strength in each of the roots of the tree. Strengths may be talents, skills or competencies. Tell them they can add more roots if they need them.

5 When they have finished the roots, ask the participants to write in each fruit a life or work success. Again, tell them they can add more if they need to.

6 When they have finished, ask the participants to exchange completed trees with a partner and discuss the relationship between their strengths and their successes.

7 Let the discussion run among the participants. Explain that they can add more strengths and successes if they come up in the discussion.

✏
✏
✏

What to look out for

Players who have trouble identifying strengths or successes. Work with them one-on-one to elicit some examples and get them going.

✏
✏
✏

Debrief

Sample debrief questions

- Did you learn anything about what makes you successful?
- Are there other successes your strengths can generate?
- What did you learn about yourself? Your partner? Your possibilities and the possibilities of other people?

✏

✏

✏

Variations

You can use the roots and fruits metaphor for any cause–result relationship. For example, company strengths and successes, or company weaknesses and failures. Roots could be mentors; fruits, life activities. There are endless applications.

Roots and fruits

Did We Learn Anything?

40 minutes	12 minimum	Content reinforcer

Why it works for me

Simple, fun way to revise with scope for a bit a laughter. Often participants start acting like they are on Jeopardy. It's wonderful when people get everything right. It also demonstrates that you have done adequate preparation as a trainer.

Where it works best

In groups that like a contest, especially more junior ones. Brightens up a technical topic but is still information focused.

What you have to do

1 Prepare in advance revision questions graded by topic and point value, and a chart showing what questions are available (see following page).

2 Break up the participants into groups of four.

3 Ask them to choose a team name.

4 Put the groups in an order around the room so they can take turns at answering questions.

5 Read out your prepared question when a team selects a topic and point value. (For example, 'Topic A for 500 please'.)

   • The team should respond with the answer.
   • Allow participants to refer to their notes.
   • Questions should be harder as the point value increases.
   • If the team answers wrongly, the question goes to the next team.

6 Keep score at the front of the room.

7 Announce the winning team when you have asked all the questions.

What to look out for

- Teams that don't know anything (try to create groups with a good mix of knowledge standards).
- Players who get too rowdy.

✏️

✏️

✏️

Debrief

Key debrief idea

Highlight strong and weak areas, and by doing so reinforce the content of the weak areas.

Sample debrief questions

- What did you know well?
- What did you forget from the session?
- Where do you need to do some more training or revision?
- Why do you think you didn't remember that information?
- What did you do to make it easy to remember some things?

✏️

✏️

✏️

Variations

- Run many small versions during the day.
- Get one team to prepare six questions for another team—this makes the game much shorter.
- Add a topic of silly questions like 'Can you name the seven dwarfs?'
- Use toy buzzers and offer joke prizes.
- Don't allow participants to refer to notes.
- Allow one of the participants to be quiz master.

Areas of the course

Topic A	Topic B	Topic C	Topic D
100	100	100	100
200	200	200	200
300	300	300	300
400	400	400	400
500	500	500	500
1000	1000	1000	1000

Point score

Anagrams

10 minutes	Any number	Content reinforcer

Why it works for me

Quick, energetic way of reinforcing main points.

What you have to do

1 Prepare some brightly coloured cards with anagrams of the key points of the session (see next page for some examples).

2 Display the cards on a wall, table or the floor.

3 Ask the participants to gather round and solve them cooperatively.

What to look out for

• Anagrams that are too easy or too hard.
• One person who is very quick and who spoils it for others.

Debrief

Sample debrief questions

• We can see what the main points are. Is there anything we've missed?
• Is there anything you should have covered that you didn't?
• What do you think should be your next step in dealing with these ideas?

Variations

• Divide into teams and compete to see who finishes first.
• Use crossword clues or mixtures of pictures and letters instead of anagrams.

Anagrams examples

Five qualities you need for a good telephone voice

saeltrens

sicentitsnsd

letasneasnps

lntsocarveoina neot

sixvrpsesesene

The answers to the above, by the way, are:

alertness
distinctness
pleasantness
conversational tone
expressiveness

Paper Aeroplane Game

10 minutes	Any number	Listening

Why it works for me

It's a creative, interactive activity with movement—a good kinaesthetic state change and role-breaker.

What you have to do

1 Give each participant a blank piece of paper.

2 Tell them it is so simple they can do it with their eyes shut. Ask them to keep their eyes closed.

3 Make sure their eyes are closed.

4 Tell them you can't answer any questions.

5 Say:

 • Fold the sheet of paper in half vertically.
 • Open the sheet and fold the top left- and right-hand corners into the centre.
 • Refold the paper in half vertically.
 • Put the paper on the desk with the first fold towards you.
 • Still holding the paper the same way, fold the near top half of the sheet towards you, and the far top half of the sheet away from you
 • Before you open your eyes, raise your hand if you've followed all the instructions.
 • Open your eyes and check that your sheet is identical to that of the person next to you. If they're not, raise your hands.

What to look out for

Keep the instructions fast enough to make following them a challenge.

Debrief

Key debrief idea

Importance of clear communication, feedback and using several senses.

Sample debrief questions

- Why do you think you all had different results?
- What was missing from the process? (feedback)
- How does feedback help you in doing your job?
- What problems arise when you don't have it?
- How can you ensure messages you send are received as you intended? (feedback, monitoring through senses)
- Do the words we use affect how well we do things? How?

Variations

- Change the instruction to 'Make a paper plane' and allow participants to make a ball of paper. This involves their creativity and listening skills.
- Use one large group or other group sizes, and involve teams and competition to complicate the communication.

Are You Listening?

5 minutes	Any number	Creativity/listening

Why it works for me

Quick and simple game that requires people to think laterally and to listen more closely than usual. It's rare that people get the answer because they switch off when listening. When they do, quite often they hide their solution, which is also something to debrief on.

Where it works best

Do it in a large group, or in pairs to develop teamwork.

What you have to do

1 Prepare handouts for every participant (see following page).

2 Explain that the game is a short word game.

3 Distribute the handouts and ask the participants to form a word by taking out four letters.

4 Repeat exactly the same instructions. Do NOT clarify.

5 After giving the participants some time to struggle, give them the hint: It's a food eaten by vegetarians.

6 After a minute stop and debrief.

✎

✎

✎

What to look out for

If the group feels you conned them by giving unclear instructions, respond by saying the exercise was about creativity, not listening, and debrief on that.

✎

✎

✎

Debrief

Key debrief ideas

1 Lateral thinking.

2 Listening to repeated instructions rather than switching off.

Sample debrief questions

- How many of you saw the solution straight away?
- What allowed you to see it?
- Even though you heard the instruction more than once, why didn't the solution appear?
- What change did you have to make to see the solution?
- How does lateral thinking help problem solving?
- How many of you got the answer and then kept quiet?
- Why do you think you didn't want to share the information?
- What happens when we don't share information?

Variations

Put the puzzle on an overhead—people can see the solution must faster.

Are You Listening? worksheet

F O L E U R N L T E T I L T E S R S

The answer to the above:

LENTILS NEEDS TO BE PRINTED

Pick the Sound

20 minutes	Any number	Listening skills

Why it works for me

A simple, fun way of reinforcing what active listening involves and that it can be difficult to do well.

Where it works best

Good for training rooms with limited space for games. Can work with almost any audience.

What you have to do

1 Collect objects that make different sounds when dropped on a hard surface. Keep them hidden from the participants. These could be, for example:

   - coins
   - phone book
   - hubcap
   - pen
   - car keys
   - umbrella
   - shoe.

2 Ask the participants to close their eyes and face away from you.

3 Ask them to guess (silently) what each item is when you drop it.

4 Drop all the items, one after another, before you get them to answer.

5 Ask them to write down their guesses.

6 Award a small prize for the most correct answers.

✎

✎

✎

What to look out for

- People who have seen your collection.
- People who call out their guesses.
- People who don't see the relevance. Remember, introduce and debrief well.

✎

✎

✎

Debrief

Key debrief idea

Listening requires concentration and an ability to interpret what we hear.

Sample debrief questions

- Did anyone find this particularly difficult? Why? What did you learn about listening from the game?
- What makes listening different from hearing? (interpreting and understanding)
- How is listening important in communication? How can it help in our everyday lives? At work?

✑

✑

✑

Variations

- Drop and guess one item at a time.
- Use CDs with sound effects or parts of songs.
- Blindfold people as well.

End with a Bang!

15 minutes	12 or more	Listening skills/teamwork

Why it works for me

This is a body-movement based game that's a lot of fun and gets people standing. At the same time, it's a conscious convincer of team building and a good example of what unexpected things people can achieve together.

Where it works best

In a group that's been together for a couple of days, when content begins to drag, or in a group that has responded well to music. It also works well when a participant is the facilitator. The environment should be a wooden floor; if on carpet, put down sheets of butcher's paper to add a feature.

What you have to do

1 Invite participants to stand in a circle and to stay quiet.

2 Tell the participants that:

- the idea of the game is to build up the sounds of the activities until they reach a crescendo (a storm at its peak)
- the activity the leader starts is passed from one participant to another in a clockwise direction, each participant continuing to make the sound
- they can only start the activity when it has been passed on to them by the person on their right
- once it has gone around the circle the leader changes the sound to one that is louder, and the process is repeated.

3 Ask the leader to begin with an activity that makes little sound (for example, rubbing hands together).

4 Ask the participants to copy it and pass it on by nodding.

5 The activities are then played in the reverse order as the storm loses its force and gradually passes.

The following activities are only a guide and can be substituted with anything the leader believes will create the same effect.

rubbing hands together	→	clicking fingers
making a 'shhh' sound	→	slapping thighs
stamping feet	→	stop stamping feet
stop slapping thighs	→	stop 'shhh' sound
stop clicking fingers	→	stop rubbing hands together
stop all activity	→	silence

What to look out for

- Have enough practice runs before you do it.
- Make sure the sound moves fast enough around the circle.
- Make sure people do not talk.
- Make sure you explain the point clearly (even if the point is simply to have fun or re-energise to aid learning).

Debrief

Sample debrief questions

- What did you have to do to make the sound develop properly? (work together)
- What did you notice yourself doing and listening to?
- How did you feel making so much noise with such a small effort?
- How did that happen? (teamwork)

Variations

- Provide musical instruments.
- Use nonsense sounds and grunts.

Author profile

Jeff Stibbard, one of Australia's leading training presenters, has a client list covering many of our biggest corporations. Over the decade he has been a professional presenter, he has developed a reputation for engaging sales and management training, for both in-house and public seminars.

After studying Psychology and Education at Sydney University, Jeff worked in face-to-face selling, training and organisational development, until choosing a career in corporate training. Along the way he collected university qualifications in both business and accounting.

He began his training career with one of the most innovative of Australian institutions, Yellow Pages Australia. This time provided the foundation for establishing his own training consultancy, Discover Performance Pty Ltd. Drawing on advanced studies in accelerated learning and change management, extensive training knowledge and wide-ranging practical experience in business, Jeff has developed and delivers courses in management, teamwork, sales and trainer's training.

He has presented to thousands of participants, in hundreds of corporate settings, and worked with many leading Australian and international presenters. It is this level of training and experience, as well as the chance to work with leading training minds, that has put Jeff in a position to communicate innovative training techniques to other trainers.

For more information

If you'd like more information about Jeff Stibbard's books, tapes and live training programs, please fill out the form below and send it to the address or fax number below:

Discover Performance Pty Ltd
PO Box 390
Surry Hills NSW 2010

Phone: 1300 135 818
Fax: 1300 135 828
E-mail: discperf@bigpond.com
Web site: www.discoverperformance.com

- -

I am interested in:

- ☐ Jeff Stibbard's seminar and conference presentations
- ☐ Live training programs with Jeff Stibbard
- ☐ In-house presentations and training consultancy with Jeff Stibbard
- ☐ Other books by Jeff Stibbard
- ☐ Tapes and training resources from Jeff Stibbard

Name

Company

Address

Postcode

Phone (Work)

Fax

Mobile

E-mail